COLORADO
MOUNTAIN CLUB
PACK GUIDE

THE BEST Buena Vista and Salida HIKES

PENELOPE PURDY

The Colorado Mountain Club Press
Golden, Colorado

PUBLISHED BY
The Colorado Mountain Club Press
15605 W. 32nd Avenue, Golden, CO 80401
303-996-2743 e-mail: cmcpress@cmc.org

Founded in 1912, the Colorado Mountain Club is the largest outdoor recreation, education, and conservation organization in the Rocky Mountains. Look for our books at your local bookstore or outdoor retailer or online at www.cmcpress.org.

CORRECTIONS: We greatly appreciate when readers alert us to errors or outdated information by emailing cmcpress@cmc.org.

Penelope Purdy: author and photographer
Erika Arroyo: designer
Jodi Jennings: copy editor
Elle Klock: production assistant

COVER PHOTO: Mount Princeton's summit ridge towers over fragile wildflowers clinging to the peak's windswept flanks. Photo by Penelope Purdy.

DISTRIBUTED TO THE BOOK TRADE BY
Mountaineers Books, 1001 SW Klickitat Way, Suite 201,
Seattle, WA 98134, 800-553-4453, www.mountaineersbooks.org

We gratefully acknowledge the financial support of the people of Colorado through the Scientific and Cultural Facilities District of greater Denver for our publishing activities.

TOPOGRAPHIC MAPS created with Gaia GPS software.

WARNING: Although there has been an effort to make the trail descriptions in this book as accurate as possible, some discrepancies may exist between the text and the trails in the field. Hiking in the mountains involves some risks. This guidebook is not a substitute for your experience and common sense. The users of this guidebook assume full responsibility for their own safety. Weather, terrain conditions, and individual technical abilities must be considered before undertaking any of the routes in this guide.

ISBN 978-1-7333321-3-2

Printed in China

24 25 / 10 9 8 7 6 5 4 3 2

OVERVIEW MAP

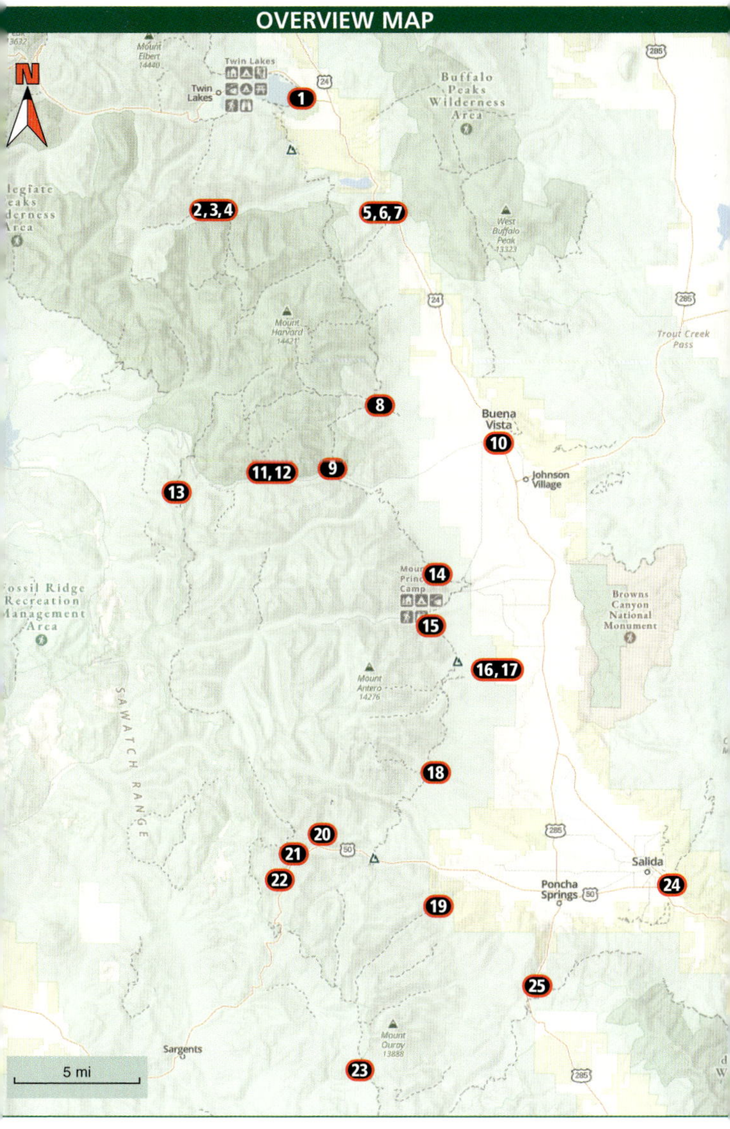

CONTENTS

THE HIKES

Front Range visitors see a classic view of Mount Princeton as they travel US 285 into the Upper Arkansas River Valley.

The Three Apostles peek over the shoulder of Mount Huron.

Introduction

This guide covers a wonderful swath of the Colorado mountains: the Upper Arkansas River Valley from Colorado Highway 82 in the north to Poncha Pass in the south; then from Trout Creek Pass in the east to the Continental Divide in the west. This scenic valley rightfully remains an ever-popular paradise for people who love the great outdoors. Several hikes are in the Collegiate Peaks section of the Sawatch Range (part of the continent-long Rocky Mountains); others are near Poncha Pass, Monarch Pass, Methodist Mountain, or the Arkansas Hills; and several are along US 50 or CO 82. This guide also notes where to find birds, wildflowers, and wildlife, as well as opportunities for fishing.

SPEAK LIKE A COLORADAN

Tabeguache Peak is pronounced "TAB-a-watch." The name refers to part of the Ute tribe who previously inhabited this beautiful valley.

Mount Ouray (a prominent high 13er) honors the great Ute chief Ouray ("you-RAY," although residents of the eponymous southwest Colorado town pronounce it "Yuri"). Chipeta, Ouray's wife, was also a respected Ute leader, and her name adorns a nearby 13er. Shavano and Antero were great Ute chiefs, too; their names are affixed to two 14ers.

A "14er" is a mountain measuring more than 14,000 feet above sea level. Colorado has at least 53 or 54, or maybe 58, depending on different interpretations of whether high summits are considered separate peaks instead of sub-summits. A "13er" is a mountain over 13,000 feet above sea level; Colorado has more than 600 "13ers." The "Centennial Peaks" are the all the 14ers plus the 13ers over 13,800 feet in elevation.

The Arkansas River passes Buena Vista, as seen from the Whipple Trail.

Coloradans pronounce the Arkansas River as "ARK-an-saw," just like the state of Arkansas. If you say "Ar-KANSAS," you're probably from Kansas. Or, like the locals, you can just call it the "Ark."

Seventeenth-century French missionaries named the river after what they called some Indigenous peoples on the southern Great Plains, and the appellation stuck as French fur trappers followed the big stream west. Thus, a river that starts in Colorado's mountains shares a name with a state hundreds of miles away.

Other area names (including the word Colorado, meaning red) are Spanish. In that language, Buena Vista is said "BWAY-na Vista," meaning beautiful view. Some locals instead call it "BEW-na Vista" because, they insist, doing so emphasizes the "beautiful" location. A few Spanish speakers have told me, though, that the mangled pronunciation disrespects their language. You can avoid the debate by using Colorado slang and calling the place "BV."

Locals pronounce Salida as "Sa-LIE-duh" although the Spanish word, which roughly translates to exit, is said "Sa-LEE-duh." It's said that the placename refers to the Arkansas River canyon gateway, through which the river appears to pour or exit from.

ABBREVIATIONS

This guide uses abbreviations for the governmental agencies that manage the lands through which hiking trails travel. The US Forest Service is shortened to "the Forest Service." Colorado Parks and Wildlife manages fishing, hunting, and wildlife habitats and is noted as "CPW." The US Bureau of Land Management is "BLM."

The Colorado Trail is designated "CT," and the Continental Divide Trail is "CDT."

WATER TALK

When Coloradans say "Divide," we're talking about the Continental Divide—the geographical separation that runs the length of the Rocky Mountains—not mathematics. The Divide's importance to the region flows from the direction in which its waters travel.

In Colorado and most Western states, the legal right to use water goes to the first person to make a claim on a stream or river. Because Colorado was settled later than its surrounding states, it doesn't get to keep all the water that originates here. For example, Kansas, Oklahoma, and Arkansas claim much of the Ark's water, which flows to the east of the Divide and drops into the Mississippi River, ultimately continuing to the Gulf of Mexico and the Atlantic Ocean.

Rivers that start on the Sawatch Range's west side flow into the Colorado River, which formerly ran into the Gulf of California and ultimately the Pacific Ocean. However, the Colorado River usually isn't able to complete its journey because so many farms and cities in Colorado, Utah, Nevada, and California use up its water along the way.

For 102 miles—from Leadville through Buena Vista and Salida—the Arkansas River is a Gold Medal fishery; at times, biologists have counted nearly 5,000 trout per mile here.

PEOPLE AND PLACES

For thousands of years, Indigenous peoples thrived in the Upper Arkansas River Valley; in winter, they resided on the warm valley floor, and during summer they followed game animals into the high country. In recent centuries, the Apache, Cheyenne, and Ute peoples also flourished here—and still reside in Colorado.

Although Spanish names dot the valley, the first Europeans here were French, mostly trappers seeking beavers whose pelts supplied the fashionable European top hat market starting in about 1830. They killed so many beavers that the species almost disappeared from Colorado. Fortunately, European fashions changed in about 1870, and a keystone Colorado species survived. Look for beaver dams along the area's creeks. These nature-made waterworks are crucial in supporting diverse wildlife, including trout, waterfowl, butterflies, and moose.

Permanent white settlers arrived around 1858, after pioneers found gold near present-day Denver. In just a few years, some 100,000 newcomers poured into what's now Colorado. Buena Vista wasn't a mining settlement but instead supplied the rough-and-tough miners who came to town for food and tools before getting drunk at any of BV's (at the time) sixty-eight taverns. But twenty years after the gold rush started, the boom went bust. The miners drifted away, leaving behind ghost towns like St. Elmo, Winfield, and Vicksburg.

Meanwhile, an unhappy chapter in Colorado history unfolded as conflicts erupted between Indigenous peoples and the new settlers. By 1868, the state and federal governments had forced Native communities to relocate, leaving the Arkansas River Valley largely bereft of its original peoples.

AVOIDING THE GHOST TOWN TRAP

Buena Vista survived its gold mining crash because smart townspeople invited railroad companies to build tracks into the valley, enabling farmers to ship their crops and livestock to market. In 1879, BV became a "real" town with the construction of a small church. (In the late twentieth century, BV residents built a new church, then spent decades arguing over what to do with the old one; they ultimately put it in a town park, where it's now a community center.)

Salida, founded in 1880 with the railroad's arrival, now has a bigger population than BV and is Chaffee County's seat. Visitors may notice that many older Salida buildings are brick: they're the second and third iterations of the community, erected after catastrophic fires in 1886 and 1888. Today, Salida's historic district includes 111 buildings on the National Historic Register.

TREES, FEATHERS, AND CRITTERS

In Colorado, entire ecosystems, including plants, birds, and wildlife, vary with altitude. Inside the larger ecosystem,

In 1879, Buena Vista began construction of this church, which today serves as the visitor center.

microecosystems form in places that hold water in summer or receive winter sunshine.

Generally, temperatures drop two degrees Fahrenheit for every 1,000 feet of elevation gain. Factor in the wind, and the weather can feel far worse at 12,000 feet than at 8,000 feet. Higher elevation also generally means snow arrives earlier and stays longer, creating spring runoff and rejuvenating the creeks, lakes, and rivers.

The Arkansas River is "the Ark" figuratively as well as literally. By providing surface water and recharging groundwater,

The Krummholz zone marks the transition from montane to alpine near the CDT.

it slakes the thirst of surrounding wildlife; supports aquatic species (insects as well as amphibians and fish); and creates riparian habitat with sedges, willows, and flowers. In the lower valley, native cottonwoods grow along the river and its tributaries, feeding and sheltering birds and small mammals. Songbirds, ouzels (water dippers), and sometimes ospreys can be found in these riparian ecosystems.

From where it emerges just west of Leadville at an elevation of over 10,000 feet, the Arkansas River meanders through a wide, relatively lush mountain valley filled with wetlands, floodplains, meadows, pastures, and hayfields. About twelve miles after it starts, the river squeezes through a tight spot formed by the Mosquito Range to the east and the Collegiate Peaks to the west, turning the waterway's gentle character into faster whitewater. This canyon belongs to mountain lions, mountain sheep, and raptors.

A hundred or so feet above the river, the ground becomes drier, forming a kind of high-altitude steppe and supporting plants such as sagebrush and pinyon pines, birds like jays and juncos, and small mammals such as jackrabbits.

As the land rises from about 9,000 feet to 11,000 feet above sea level, it gets more winter snow and retains it later into spring. Cooler weather and abundant water create a montane ecosystem marked by aspen, ponderosa and lodgepole pine, Douglas fir, blue spruce (Colorado's state tree), and Engelmann spruce. Early summer wildflowers such as blue Columbine (Colorado's state flower) blanket meadows and forest floors. The montane ecosystem is home to iconic black bears and elk. Common birds here include nuthatches (listen for their characteristic *yak-yak* echoing through the trees) and (one of my favorites) the modestly colored hermit thrush, which sings one of nature's most glorious tunes. Most hikes described in this book travel partly or entirely through the montane ecosystem.

At about 11,000 feet, the montane surrenders to subalpine ecosystems and the weird world of the Krummholz zone. Here, endless winds and harsh winters twist and stunt vegetation into a kind of natural bonsai garden—even small trees may be hundreds of years old. Hardy perennial grasses, forbs, cushion plants, and mosses hunker down among the sparse tree cover. Take care when traveling through this fragile zone.

Life maintains its toehold above timberline on Mount Princeton.

Timberline in the Sawatch Range starts at elevations from 11,000 and 12,000 feet. Here, trees cannot grow in the long, fierce winters, which (historically) have resembled Arctic conditions. Still, mammals such as marmots and pika thrive here, along with birds like the ground-dwelling ptarmigan, which turns brown in summer and white in winter. In the short weeks between snowmelt and winter's return, the alpine tundra blooms with small, gorgeous flowers such as sky pilot, blue forget-me-nots, white phlox, and pink moss campion. Marsh marigolds and yellow buttercups emerge near melting snowbanks both at timberline and in the montane zone. Stay on the trail here because the alpine ecosystem can be destroyed by a careless human footstep. This eco-zone is, sadly, the most vulnerable to human-caused climate change.

WHITEWATER

A boater needs a bombproof combat roll to safely paddle the Arkansas River's Class IV/V rapids. If you lack that skill, or worse, you didn't understand that sentence, you need to hire a guide or join a commercial raft trip to explore the Ark in this valley. Several state-licensed river adventure companies have permits to operate on the Ark. Check online and ask locals for

Clad in full safety gear, an expert kayaker plays in the Ark's rapids on a moderate-level day on the river. At higher waters, the Ark can become dangerous.

recommendations. Whitewater paddling can be loads of fun, but the Ark is never tame.

FISHING FACTS

The Buena Vista/Salida area is trout-fishing heaven, mostly for rainbow, brown, cutthroat, and brookies. To sustain this remarkable fishery and the ecosystems that depend on it, we all need to play by the rules.

Any angler age 16 or older needs a valid license to fish in Colorado. Adults ages 18 to 64 pay full cost. Youths ages 16 to 17, seniors over age 64, and people with low incomes pay discounted prices. Residents pay less than nonresidents. (A state resident is a person who has lived in Colorado continuously for six months or more.) Both residents and nonresidents can buy licenses for anywhere from one day to one year. All adults must present legally valid identification (such as a current driver's license) to buy a fishing license. CPW adjusts prices or otherwise modifies its rules annually. For up-to-date information, visit https://cpw.state.co.us.

CPW further requires anglers to use only artificial lures and flies in most area streams and lakes, including the Ark. Many fisheries here also are "catch and release," so all fish in these designated waters must be returned to the water, unharmed, as quickly as possible. CPW allows "catch and eat" in a few lakes and streams but restricts how many fish any angler can keep in a day (bag or creel limits). Most area anglers use fly rods.

A NOTE ABOUT CLIMATE CHANGE

According to the Associated Press's expert science writer, scientists are as sure that humans are causing climate change as they are about the link between cigarette smoking and lung cancer.[1] Even now, Colorado is suffering worse than just

---

1 Seth Borenstein, "Climate Change as Certain as Cancer from Smoking, Scientists Say." HeraldNet.com, September 24, 2013. www.heraldnet.com/news/climate-change-as-certain-as-cancer-from-smoking-scientists-say/

A 2019 fire charred the forest along the Rainbow Trail's eastern edge.

another drought, with the state's entire climate becoming more arid. High-country ecosystems already have shifted, putting pika and other wildlife at risk. In the montane zones, warmer winters now enable two or three generations of pine bark beetles to hatch each year. Previously, just one generation hatched annually. Thus, battalions of bark-burrowing bugs already have turned many Colorado forests gray or rust-colored.

The most visible proof of climate change is the emergence of the "megafires," blazes so massive and fast-moving that they're almost unstoppable. The largest Colorado wildfires in recorded history all happened in the twenty-first century, with three occurring in 2020. One fire, aptly named East Troublesome Fire, blew up 100,000 acres of forest in a single day, an event that experienced wildland fire fighters called "terrifying." And forests in the Upper Arkansas River Valley face similar risks.

BIRTH OF THE ROCKIES

Scientists estimate that our world is about four billion years old, but most of Earth's original rocks did not survive the planet's early eons, when the infant world was a seething ball of molten rock bombarded by debris from the toddler solar system. Earth still has a molten core, which is good, because the magnetic field it creates saves our atmosphere from being ripped away by the powerful solar wind. But the active core also means that our planet is a work in progress.

The molten core likely is the power source that makes continents and their tectonic plates move slowly around the globe. When the plates collide, earthquakes and volcanoes happen,

The floor of the Upper Arkansas River Valley is slowly being pulled apart.

and deep ocean trenches and mountains are formed. Almost all of these processes and features occur in proximity to the edges of continental plates.

But the 3,000-mile-long Rocky Mountains (numerous strung-together ranges that stretch from northern Canada through the United States and into Mexico) are hundreds of miles from the present-day edge of the North American continent. So why do the Rockies exist?

Earth scientists suspect that millions of years ago some force slowed the Pacific Plate where it plunges under North America, and the excessive friction and pressure crinkled the continent far inland. Other possibilities include a geological weakness that may underlie North America, bending the land; or maybe the plate's boundary shifted over geologic time.

In fact, today's Rockies are the third mountain range to rise in what now is Colorado. The oldest rocks in the Upper Arkansas River Valley date to the Precambrian time, about 1.7 billion to 1.8 billion years ago. Most are types of granite—metamorphic rock "recycled" through the Earth and pushed to the surface again—that predate the present Rockies by about 100 million years.

Those earlier mountains succumbed to the long, slow forces of erosion, but they left their calling cards in today's exposed rock layers. Erosion also removed most of the sedimentary rock cover, sending thick deposits of sandstone and shale into adjacent basins. During the next several hundred million years (the Paleozoic period), shallow seas swept into the land and retreated multiple times.

The Rockies we know today resulted from a famous geologic event called the Laramide Orogeny, which began about 80 million years ago and continued in fits until about 55 million years ago. Along the Front Range, evidence of the Orogeny is seen in the Red Rocks Amphitheater and the Boulder Flatirons; both are part of the Fountain Formation, the red sandstone that tilted skyward as the Rockies rose. In the Upper Arkansas River Valley, signs of the Laramide Orogeny appear in the uplifted rock layers on the high peaks and sides of canyons.

Much more recently—merely tens of thousands of years ago—several Ice Ages blanketed the Rockies. Their glaciers carved U-shaped valleys, such as the "chair" formation on Mount Ouray. They also left behind towering deposits of boulders and gravel called moraines, and dropped big, oddly placed boulders called "erratics."

During these Ice Ages, violent natural dramas performed three times near the valley's northern side, most likely starting near the present-day Pine Creek and Clear Creek drainages. Huge glaciers created massive ice dams and formed lakes 600 feet deep and about 100 miles long. Then the ice dams collapsed catastrophically, sending a titanic flood roaring southward, buzz-sawing a deep channel through hard rock walls and randomly depositing massive boulders. Evidence of this ancient, roaring cataclysm today flanks US 24 through the narrow canyon near the hamlet of Granite.

THE SAWATCH TODAY

The Sawatch Range, which towers over the valley's west side, has fifteen peaks with elevations above 14,000 feet. The southernmost 14ers—Shavano, Tabeguache, Antero, and Princeton—formed from the same big blob of granite shoved skyward by the Laramide Orogeny. But over time, wind, water, and gravity worked a natural origami: today, alluvial fans stretch eastward dozens of miles from the mountains. Between Nathrop and Salida, US 285 undulates over ridges and through streambeds that were molded and carved by erosion's irresistible power.

On the valley's east side, the Arkansas Hills' sandy soil comes from ground-down granite, the same rock seen in the crazy-shaped crags. Ice Age glaciers didn't reach this far; these formations result from the action of water and wind. These lower hills also are drier than the much higher peaks to the west.

The long, U-shaped Pine Creek valley shows classic signs of Ice Age glaciation.

Complex forces built the valley's southern side near Salida and made the river turn sharply eastward. US 50's roadcut east through Bighorn Sheep Canyon is lined by red rocks, very different from the tans and grays that dominate the Sawatch Range. Methodist Mountain, a popular hiking and biking area south of town, actually is the northeast edge of the Sangre de Cristo Range, which has its own geologic story.

HIKING GEOLOGY'S WONDERLAND

Watch out—the ground you walk on moves! Geology's glacial pace formed the beautiful mountains, lifting and sculpting the landscape over millennia and slowly creating places for life to thrive. But geology also occurs suddenly with avalanches, flash floods, rockslides, collapsing stream beds, and stones tumbling onto trails.

Layers of rocks reveal what happened in the past, somewhat like the grain in a piece of wood can show much about the tree from which it came. Stop at the Arkansas River Valley Overlook off US 285 and Chaffee County Road 304 to view the ancient, complex, and occasionally violent story written in the landscape.

The valley floor is the northern part of the Rio Grande Rift, a ground movement that's slowly pulling North America

This massive erratic along the Pine Creek Trail sports telltale stripes or "striations" where the pressure of moving glaciers scraped across the dense rock. Note the size of the mature pines that have grown around the monolith.

apart from east to west. The rift is narrow near Leadville, expands from Buena Vista south through Salida, further widens in the San Luis Valley, and keeps growing through New Mexico and into Mexico. Despite this ceaseless stretch, the valley is strangely calm: Colorado sporadically gets small earthquakes, but none have occurred in this valley for thousands of years.

The valley sports other geologic activity, too, including hot springs near Mount Princeton, Salida, and Cottonwood Creek. Mineral-rich water rising from deep in the earth also shaped the Chalk Cliffs on Mount Princeton's south side.

THE ONGOING LEGACY

Geologic forces bequeathed Colorado abundant natural riches. In the nineteenth century, miners rushed to the Rockies searching for the gold and silver brought up from the planet's core during mountain-building times. Other settlers dug near places like Craig and Ludlow for coal, which dates to the warm and lush Carboniferous period (about 300 million years ago). In the twentieth century, wildcatters and tycoons drilled into the sediment-filled basins, searching for crude oil and natural gas.

Today, the high peaks continue to capture snow; when it melts, it sends water, the most precious resource of all, to sustain wildlife habitat and the cities, farms, and ranches downstream. Of course, without the mountains and the rivers they spawn, the state wouldn't have its ski resorts, whitewater rafting, fishing, and countless other recreational attractions. So, ponder this legacy as you venture out to enjoy these hikes!

The Ten Essentials

Always take these items with you when hiking, climbing, or doing other wilderness adventures as your life may depend on these tools. The Ten Essentials can include other items depending on the season and activity. Today's lightweight gear makes carrying these things easy—most of my essentials fit into a quart-sized, waterproof bag. Learn to "ranger roll" your warm clothing and jacket so they'll squeeze into a small daypack. Generally, the essentials are:

1. Extra food and extra water, and a way to purify any water that you find. (Take enough of both so you can have a snack when you return to your car—that means you also have enough of each to survive a night in the woods.)
2. Extra layers like a coat, hat, gloves, bandana, and of course rain jacket and rain pants. I also take an extra pair of lightweight liner socks. On high-altitude hikes, I take my ultra-lightweight bike jacket to use as a wind shirt, too.
3. Sun protection: sun hat, sunscreen, lip balm. (Add a cord or cap keeper because mountain breezes grow into mountain winds in a nanosecond.)
4. First aid kit. Know that many items, such as clothing, can double as bandages and other medical items. (And take a good wilderness first aid course!)
5. Headlamp or flashlight.
6. Knife or multitool.
7. Fire starter, both a way to make a spark and something that will flame easily. (I believe in Murphy's Law so I take all three: lighter, matches, and a flint. Lint from your clothes

dryer makes great kindling. So does lip balm grease or fat from a chocolate bar.)

8. Navigation: always take a map and compass as well as a GPS or cell phone because batteries wear out and die.
9. Signal devices, including a whistle (for audible signal) and mirror or light (for visual signal). Today's emergency communication technologies are remarkably light and affordable. (And remember my bike jacket? It's neon yellow with flecks of light-reflective material—if I wave it around on a 14er, they'll see me in the next county.)
10. Some way to make shelter such as an emergency blanket or lightweight tarp. (Basic survival classes also teach you how to use the natural resources around you. For example, how to make a lean-to out of fallen logs or how to dig a snow trench in Colorado's fluffy powder.)

And here are a few additional suggestions:

11. Situational awareness. Pay attention to what's around you, such as changing weather, rising creeks, rockfall, snow slides, and signs that predators are nearby.
12. Basic weather know-how. Most importantly, know what the Colorado mountain sky looks like before a thunderstorm develops. Understand that a shift in wind direction may warn that a cold front is on its way. Figure out how to tell temperature ranges, even if you break your thermometer. Learn how trees and waves offer clues about wind speed. Learn the different kinds of clouds and what they mean—it's fun!
13. Humility in the face of nature's power. Recognize when you've crossed the fine line between pushing yourself and taking an undue risk. It's okay to turn around—you're not storming Normandy Beach or landing an airliner on the Hudson River.

BUENA VISTA AREA

The Sawatch Range near timberline on Mount Yale.

1. Interlaken

RATING	Easy
ROUND-TRIP DISTANCE	4.7 miles
ROUND-TRIP TIME	2.5 to 3.5 hours
STARTING ELEVATION	9,230 feet
ENDING ELEVATION	9,190 feet
ELEVATION GAIN	40 feet (high point 9,270 feet)
MAPS	Trails Illustrated #110 Leadville
TRAILHEAD	Twin Lakes Interlaken Trailhead

COMMENT: This gentle trail, accessible year-round, is popular for snowshoeing as well as hiking. Many families bring youngsters here, but make sure that little ones don't toddle into the cold lake. The route undulates over small hills as it winds along a section of Twin Lakes's south shore, providing great views of the water and the surrounding peaks on the way to the historic but abandoned Interlaken Resort. The mostly shaded trail provides relief from Colorado's intense summer sun, but the same trees let snow and ice form in early fall and linger into spring; at these times, using snowshoes or traction devices is a good idea. The covered porch at Dexter's Cabin offers shade for summer picnics and a dry spot of winter warmth for a December lunch.

Dogs are allowed; leashes are recommended. Good opportunities exist for viewing birds and wildflowers, and the fall foliage display is excellent. Twin Lakes offers good fishing, but there is ice and/or snow on the trail from late October through mid-May. In summer, avoid afternoon thundershowers.

GETTING THERE: From US 24, turn west on CO 82/Independence Pass Road. (The trailhead is accessible even when the

The year-round trail to Interlaken includes splendid views of Twin Lakes.

pass is closed.) The well-marked turn onto CO 82 is about 20.0 miles south of Leadville, 34.0 miles north of Buena Vista, and 59.0 miles north of Salida. From the highway junction, drive west on CO 82 for just 0.8 mile (passing the Lost Canyon Road). Turn left (south) onto the poorly marked Lake County Road 25; as of 2020, the Aspen Rafting company's red building stood across the highway from the turn. Drive southwest on CR 25 for 0.5 mile to a junction with another dirt road. Bear left to stay on CR 25 for another 0.1 mile. (In mid-winter, two-wheel-drive cars may have to park near here.) The county road passes an unnamed dirt road and then reaches a second dirt road. At this second unnamed dirt road, turn right and uphill; the parking area and markers for the CT are on your left.

THE HIKE: Walk toward the metal gate with CT and CDT markers on its post. Almost immediately, leave the road and look for another CT marker to your right. Turn onto the CT and follow the foot path into the trees. Continue for 1.3 miles as the trail meanders up and down small slopes, mostly staying near the lake. At 1.3 miles at a marked intersection, the trail

Hikers find informational signs that relate the history of Interlaken.

splits, with the newer CT link heading uphill and left. Don't turn, but instead continue straight on the westbound old CT nearer the lake. Walk another 0.9 mile to a second junction with another CT link that heads left and uphill. Once more, don't turn, but continue straight for just over 0.1 mile to the Interlaken site. Camping and campfires are prohibited near the historic area, but a few dispersed camping sites can be found along the trail.

At the abandoned Interlaken Resort, the historic cabin's porch still provides a pleasant perch for a picnic in summer or winter.

82
25
Twin Lakes Dam
The Colorado Trail
TRAILHEAD
2000 ft
Mountain View Fishing Site
9800
Interlaken Historic Resort
N

2. Mount Huron

RATING	Difficult; Class 2 and rocky above timberline; weather exposure
ROUND-TRIP DISTANCE	11.0 miles (from the two-wheel-drive parking); 6.75 miles (from the four-wheel-drive parking)
ROUND-TRIP TIME	6 to 7.5 hours (from the two-wheel-drive parking); 3.5 to 5 hours (from the four-wheel-drive parking)
STARTING ELEVATION	10,200 feet (two-wheel-drive parking); 10,600 feet (four-wheel-drive parking)
ENDING ELEVATION	14,003 feet
ELEVATION GAIN	3,800 feet (from the end of the two-wheel-drive road); 3,400 feet (from the end of four-wheel-drive road)
MAPS	Trails Illustrated #129 Buena Vista/ Collegiate Peaks
TRAILHEAD	South Clear Creek Trailhead

COMMENT: Mount Huron is the most difficult of the high peaks described in this book, although it's not as challenging as some other 14ers. The Colorado Fourteeners Initiative fixed this trail so it's easy to follow in summer and fall, but winter and spring snows conceal the path and expose the upper reaches to avalanche hazard. In any season, however, even the well-engineered new trail remains unrelentingly steep, so it will give your quads a good workout on the way up and tax your hamstrings on the descent. Meanwhile, you'll pass through an old-growth forest, parallel a rushing mountain stream, and see marvelous views of surrounding peaks and valleys. The scenery and varied ecosystems make the significant effort worthwhile for moderate to experienced hikers.

Dogs are allowed on leash. Bird viewing is good, as is wildflower viewing in early summer. Fall foliage is excellent. Fishing is allowed only in Clear Creek (near the access road) or the South Fork (across from the four-wheel-drive parking). Note that this trail is weather-exposed, and avalanche hazard exists from late fall to late spring.

GETTING THERE: A four-wheel-drive vehicle shortens the approach considerably. From US Highway 24, go west at a brown sign for Chaffee County Road 390/Clear Creek Road. This intersection is about 14.5 miles north of Buena Vista and 20.0 miles south of Leadville. Pass the state wildlife area and follow CR 390, a dirt road friendly to passenger cars, for almost 12.0 miles, driving by historic sites and trails to other 14ers along the way. Reach the old mining site of Winfield. At the ghost town's west end, turn left at an intersection and cross the creek on a good bridge. Almost immediately after the bridge, two-wheel-drive cars should park either in the pullouts along the road or in the big lot on the road's left.

The route up Mount Huron follows cairns across the tundra, left of the cliffs, then ascends the ramp and climbs to Huron's summit.

Views near timberline on Mount Huron include a long look down the Clear Creek drainage.

Do not block the road. SUVs can drive the next 2.2 miles, and you may want to hitch a ride with one of them on the way down. Find plenty of dispersed camping spots along the four-wheel-drive road but bring your drinking water, or filter/treat what you fetch from the creek.

THE HIKE: The four-wheel-drive road ends at a locked metal gate; just after it, a wooden sign says "Mt. Huron" and points left. Step steeply up well-placed stones and ascend numerous tight switchbacks through an old-growth forest, sometimes paralleling a creek. Reach timberline at about 12,000 feet, climb through the Krummholz zone, and enter an open basin that fills with summer wildflowers. Huron's hulk looms to your right, but there's no sane way up to it from here. Instead, stay on the obvious trail and cross the basin by following cairns. Near the basin's east end, sneak left of a cliff band. Continue east for about a half mile, then reach a long, arduous slope that tilts south toward the summit. Labor upward, clattering over scree and talus. Reach the top, and whew! What a view!

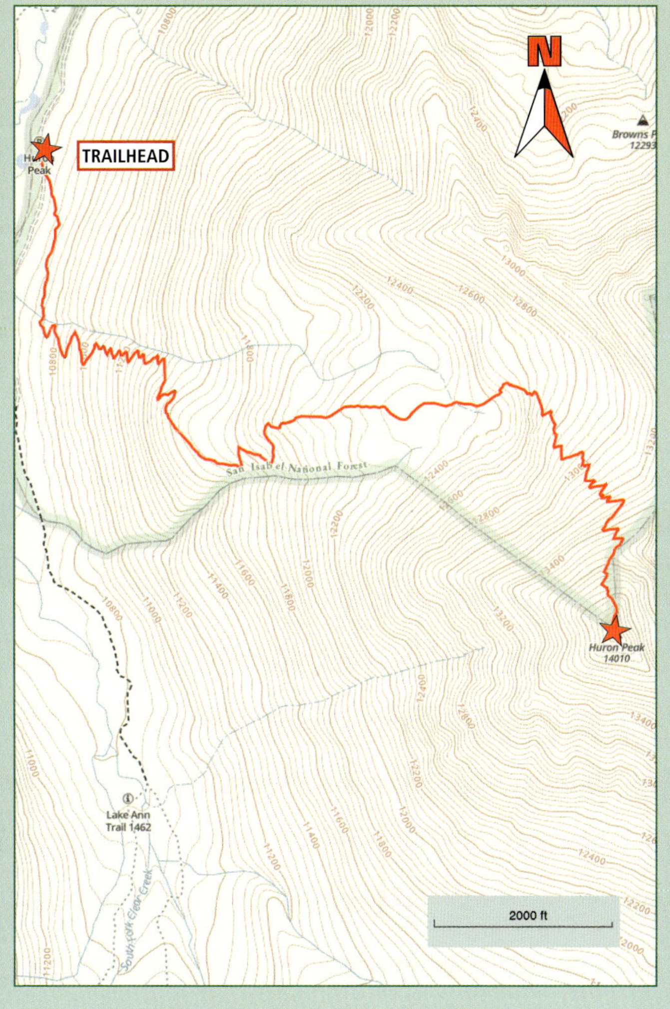
TRAILHEAD
N
Huron Peak
Huron Peak
14010
Browns P
12293
San Isabel National Forest
Lake Ann
Trail 1462
South Fork Clear Creek
2000 ft

3. Three Apostles Basin and View

RATING	Moderate
ROUND-TRIP DISTANCE	7.2 miles (from the two-wheel-drive parking); 3.0 miles (from the four-wheel-drive parking)
ROUND-TRIP TIME	3.6 to 5 hours (from the two-wheel-drive parking); 1.5 to 2.25 hours (from the four-wheel-drive parking)
STARTING ELEVATION	10,200 feet (two-wheel-drive parking); 10,600 feet (four-wheel-drive parking)
ENDING ELEVATION	11,400 feet
ELEVATION GAIN	1,200 feet (from the end of the two-wheel-drive road); 800 feet (from the end of the four-wheel-drive road)
MAPS	Trails Illustrated #129 Buena Vista/ Collegiate Peaks
TRAILHEAD	South Clear Creek Trailhead

COMMENT: Many Buena Vista area trails give glimpses of the rugged, impressive Three Apostles, but this hike takes you right to their base in a high, wetland basin that's often filled with wildflowers. The way to this dramatic cove of cathedral-like mountains is generally pleasant and exceptionally beautiful. So, enjoy the wonderful walk into the isolated basin at the foot of these steep walls of rock and ice; you don't necessarily need to climb a mountain to appreciate its grandeur.

Dogs are allowed on leash. Bird viewing opportunities are good, and wildflower/foliage viewing is excellent. Fishing is good in the creeks but not in the tarn at the base of the peaks. There is avalanche hazard from late fall to late spring.

Breathtaking vistas of jagged peaks invite hikers toward Three Apostles Basin.

GETTING THERE: A four-wheel-drive vehicle shortens the approach considerably. From US Highway 24, go west at a brown sign for Chaffee County Road 390/Clear Creek Road. This intersection is about 14.5 miles north of Buena Vista and 20.0 miles south of Leadville. Pass the state wildlife area and follow CR 390, a dirt road friendly to passenger cars, for almost 12.0 miles, driving by historic sites and trails to other 14ers along the way. Reach the old mining site of Winfield. At the ghost town's west end, turn left at an intersection and cross the creek on a good bridge. Almost immediately after the bridge, two-wheel-drive cars should park either in the pullouts along the road or in the big lot on the road's left. Do not block the road. SUVs can drive the next 2.2 miles, and you may want to hitch a ride with one of them on the way down. Find plenty of dispersed camping spots along

The Three Apostles look even more challenging close-up, while wildflowers and songbirds thrive in the lush high-altitude valley at their base.

the four-wheel-drive road but bring your drinking water, or filter/treat what you fetch from the creek.

THE HIKE: From the locked gate at the end of the four-wheel-drive road, walk straight west on the old road; do not turn onto the Mount Huron Trail. Read the sign if you're confused. The Three Apostles Trail shares the first, relatively flat 1.4 miles with the Lake Ann Trail (another great hike covered in this guide). The routes diverge before a creek crossing, where a sign points right (southwest) across the stream for Lake Ann. Don't go that way. Instead, follow the less-traveled path straight ahead. Soon after the trail junction, a side trail leads uphill to nowhere; ignore it. Continue to another creek crossing (tricky at high water) and decide if you prefer hopping rocks or balancing on logs. Once across, encounter the steepest part of the trail, a crumbling dirt slope where grabbing an occasional tree root is permissible.

Once atop the small hill, parallel a creek rushing in a deep ravine to your left. The ravine becomes shallower along the last 0.8 mile, and you can easily step across the stream near its headwaters. Now enter the remote sanctuary and find yourself at the feet of the Three Apostles, including a thriving, high altitude wetland full of flowers, sedges, and willows. Ahead steep cliffs of rock, ice, and snow rear skyward. If the weather allows, find a fallen log and enjoy lunch before returning to day-to-day reality.

Note: The Three Apostles is a technical climb, and how to accomplish this climb is beyond the scope of this book. Ice Mountain (the center Apostle) is a particularly dangerous peak. In summer and fall, most of its precariously balanced loose scree and talus is ready to roll downhill at the slightest touch. In winter and spring, Ice Mountain can release deadly avalanches. Proceed beyond timberline here with caution.

Elephantheads and wild daisies bask in the summer sun and soak up spring snowmelt in Three Apostles Basin.

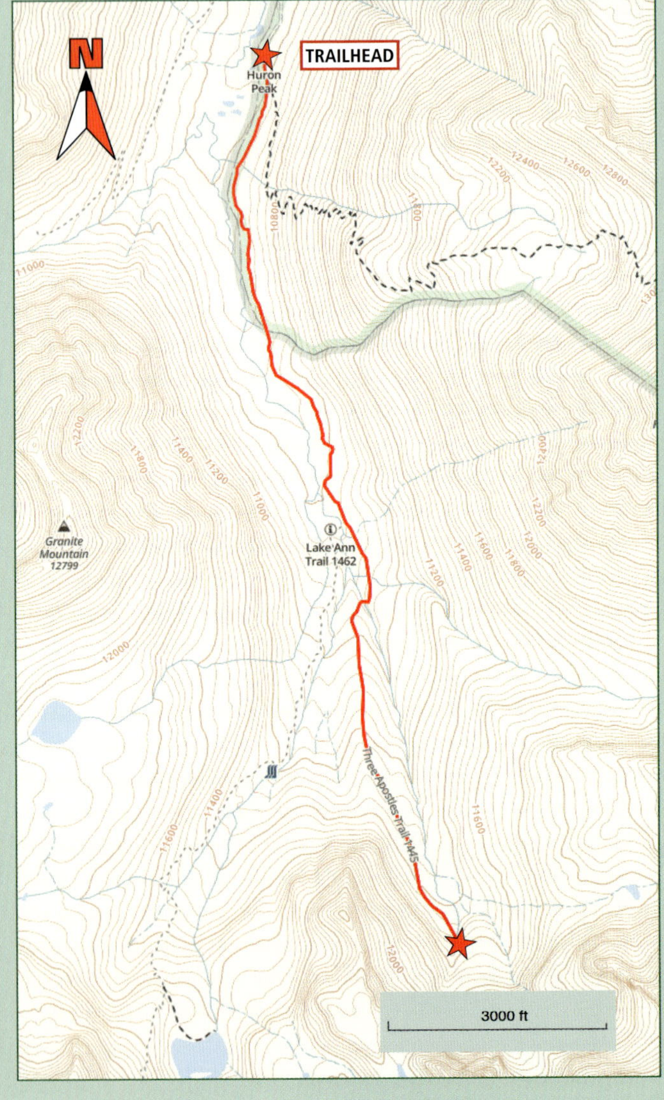
N
TRAILHEAD
Huron Peak
Granite Mountain 12799
Lake Ann Trail 1462
Three Apostles Trail 1445
3000 ft

4. Lake Ann

RATING	Moderate
ROUND-TRIP DISTANCE	11.0 miles (from the two-wheel-drive parking); 6.6 miles (from the upper four-wheel-drive parking)
ROUND-TRIP TIME	5.5 to 7.3 hours (from the two-wheel-drive parking); 3.3 to 4.5 hours (from the four-wheel-drive parking)
STARTING ELEVATION	10,200 feet (two-wheel-drive parking); 10,600 feet (four-wheel-drive parking
ENDING ELEVATION	11,800 feet
ELEVATION GAIN	1,600 feet (from the two-wheel-drive parking); 1,250 feet (from the four-wheel-drive parking)
MAPS	Trails Illustrated #129 Buena Vista/ Collegiate Peaks
TRAILHEAD	South Clear Creek Trailhead

COMMENT: Lake Ann glistens in certain sunlit hours with an amazing aquamarine hue, perhaps emanating from the quality of granite under the water. This same rock forms the escarpments that bend along three-quarters of the shoreline. South and east of the lake rise the summit dragon teeth of the Three Apostles, clear reminders that this part of the Sawatch is far more rugged and less traveled than the rest of the range. To reach this liquid gem, the trail traverses a subalpine meadow, crosses mountain streams, weaves through aspen stands, and just before the final push to timberline, enters a cathedral grove of ancient spruce. If this trailhead sat closer to the paved road many more people would wonder at its beauty, but because Lake Ann hides in a wilderness just below the Divide, fewer humans visit. Hikers coming

Lake Ann glistens like a high-altitude gem surrounded by rugged cliffs.

from the lower trailhead may want to backpack, but the Forest Service forbids camping on the fragile lake shores; it is far better to pitch a tent among the trees.

Dogs on leash are allowed. Bird, wildflower, and fall foliage viewing are excellent. Fishing is good, especially in the lake. Note that moose are in the area, and the trail is weather-exposed above timberline.

GETTING THERE: A four-wheel-drive vehicle shortens the approach considerably. From US Highway 24, go west at a brown sign for Chaffee County Road 390/Clear Creek Road. This intersection is about 14.5 miles north of Buena Vista and 20.0 miles south of Leadville. Pass the state wildlife area and follow CR 390, a dirt road friendly to passenger cars, for almost 12.0 miles, driving by historic sites and trails to other 14ers along the way. Reach the old mining site of Winfield. At the ghost town's west end, turn left at an intersection and

The Lake Ann Trail travels through old-growth forest and across high alpine tundra.

cross the creek on a good bridge. Almost immediately after the bridge, two-wheel-drive cars should park either in the pullouts along the road or in the big lot on the road's left. Do not block the road. SUVs can drive the next 2.2 miles, and you may want to hitch a ride with one of them on the way down. Find plenty of dispersed camping spots along the four-wheel-drive road but bring your drinking water, or filter/treat what you fetch from the creek.

THE HIKE: From the upper parking area, pass through the metal gate and walk 1.4 miles on the same path that leads to the Three Apostles Basin. The trail splits near a wide meadow with magnificent views of the Apostles and the Continental Divide. At the signed trail junction, leave the path of the Apostles and bear right. Cross the creek on a wooden bridge, push through a brushy area, then maneuver around avalanche debris to step over a small side stream (notice along the way how many big trees the snowslide demolished). From here, the trail climbs steadily through mature conifer forests filled, in summer, with flickers, woodpeckers, juncos, and nuthatches. At 2.8 miles, cross yet another creek on a good log bridge. The trail then drops to another stream and another bridge. Resume the upward march and enter the realm of spruce giants, pondering, perhaps, the age and persistence of this venerable grove. The ancient forest eventually surrenders to the Krummholz zone. Reach timberline, and once above the trees, keep your eyes out for wild mountain goats. At about 3.2 miles, the trail hits an unmarked Y junction. Take the left trail down 0.1 mile to the lake. The right branch leads up to the Continental Divide, so if you find yourself looking down on the gem-like lake, you've missed your turn.

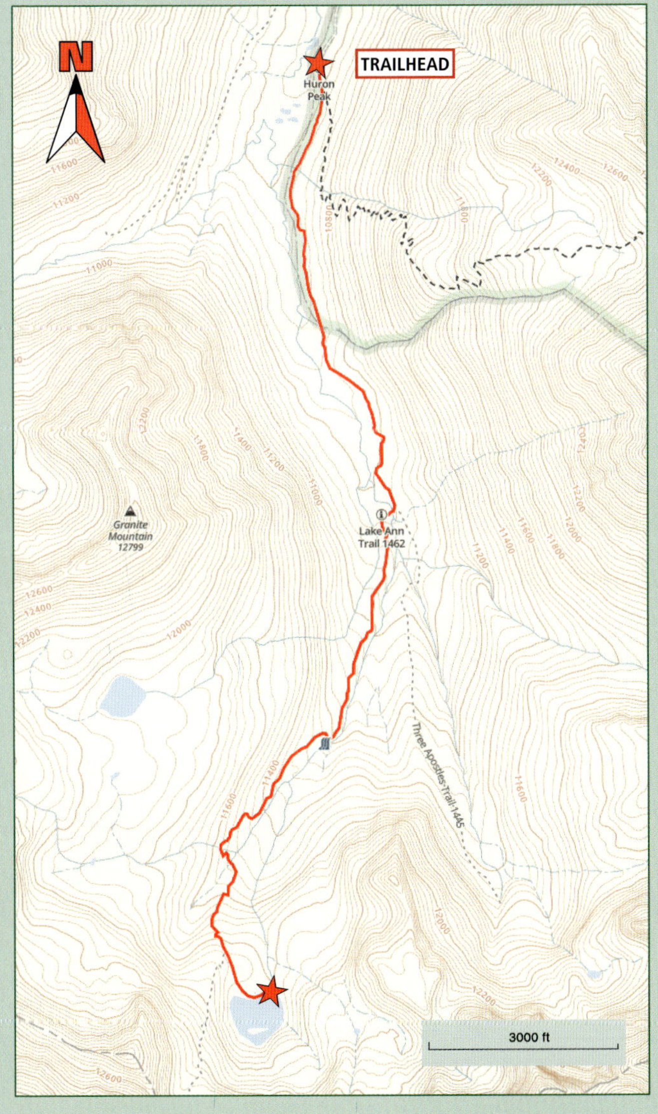

N
TRAILHEAD
Huron Peak
Granite Mountain 12799
Lake Ann Trail 1462
Three Apostles Trail 1445
3000 ft

5. Pine Creek/Bedrock Falls

RATING	Moderate
ROUND-TRIP DISTANCE	17.0 miles
ROUND-TRIP TIME	8.5 hours to 11.5 hours (backpack recommended)
STARTING ELEVATION	8,800 feet
ENDING ELEVATION	11,253 feet
ELEVATION GAIN	2,453 feet
MAPS	Trails Illustrated #129 Buena Vista/ Collegiate Peaks
TRAILHEAD	Pine Creek Trailhead

COMMENT: Pine Creek harbors more wildlife than neighboring valleys because fewer people come here. Use extra care while visiting this spectacular place, so pretend that you must earn an A+ in a Leave No Trace Master Class. The hike passes through several ecosystems and geologic eras, making the journey an extended nature walk. The trail provides access to two high 13ers, four 14ers (this guide describes two of them), and connections to the CT. It then leads to a cascade tumbling over Precambrian, or bedrock, granite.

Dogs are allowed on leash. Bird and wildlife viewing are excellent, and the fall foliage is exceptional. Fishing is also excellent. Be aware that moose and bears are in the area.

Note: You must pay a fee to cross the first mile of private land, which at the time of printing is $1 per person/$2 per animal (dog or livestock). The modest charge assures public access while preserving private property rights.

GETTING THERE: Drive US 24 to Chaffee County Road 388. This exit is 38.0 miles north of Salida, 13.7 miles from the Main Street/Cottonwood Pass stoplight in Buena Vista, 22.0 miles south of downtown Leadville, and 4.5 miles south of

Pine Creek tumbles down the Bedrock Falls.

Ice Age glaciers and possibly a massive flood left behind this giant, oddly placed boulder, called an "erratic."

Granite. Only a small, blue county road sign marks this turn, but CR 388 is north of "The Numbers" river recreation area and just south of AVA's Granite Via Ferrata. Exit the highway and drive south on CR 388 for 0.4 miles, then veer left to stay on the main road. Low-clearance passenger cars should park near the sharp curve that appears next. SUVs and high-clearance, two-wheel-drive vehicles can drive another 0.8 mile to the trailhead.

THE HIKE: Take a moment before leaving your vehicle, and look east across the highway—opposite the direction you soon will hike. US 24 in this part of the valley follows the deep cleft that massive Ice Age floods sliced through the granite. In fact, boulders left during the violent geologic past still form a major rapid in the Arkansas River about where Pine Creek flows into it. Now, with increased respect for nature's power, turn your back on the cliffs and face west to start your hike. Then pay the modest access fee and pass through the metal gate, closing it behind you. Walk 2.0 miles through a flat area where sagebrush flanks the trail, indicating an arid, high altitude steppe ecosystem. But by the creek to your right, cottonwoods and other native trees thrive near the water, providing great bird habitat. Continue trekking toward stands of ponderosa pine, among the West's most common trees. Its thick, orange-tinted bark lets it endure wildfires that periodically sweep Colorado forests. In fact, small, natural blazes encourage the growth of ponderosa seedlings. True pines produce needles in clusters; ponderosa pines sprout them in groups of three.

The trail gently climbs as it enters the lodgepole pines. These trees have needles in pairs, grayish bark, and trunks much smaller in diameter than ponderosa pines. Their sticky cones need heat to open, so lodgepole pines are a "fire adapted" species. Charring at the lodgepoles' base indicates a fire crept along the forest floor here in the recent past. Stray, enormous boulders—erratics—stand sentry near the trail. Glaciers brought these many-ton monoliths down from the high peaks then left them behind after the Ice Age retreated. The path enters a classic Colorado geologic feature, the V-shaped, stream-carved canyon. Enter the Collegiate Peaks Wilderness shortly before the trail bends right and crosses Pine Creek on a good bridge. Intersect the southbound CT, but don't turn; continue west. Now the landscape opens onto another gift of geologic magic, the big U-shaped, glacial-carved valley. The trail swings around the first beaver pond. Now meet the northbound CT but stay westbound. Good campsites exist here and throughout the valley. Notice the beaver dams left of the trail. Ponds created by the big rodents' earthworks enable many aquatic species (including trout) to thrive, while the surrounding wetlands feed big mammals (especially moose) and provide habitat for birds, bugs, and butterflies.

Beavers, which built their lodge on Pine Creek, enhance habitat for many wildlife species ranging from butterflies to moose.

At 6.5 miles, the Pine Creek path passes an antique log cabin and the left turn for the rough South Pine Creek Trail. Continue to head west on the path. Notice the higher elevation spruce-fir forest to the right, evidencing a montane ecosystem. The wide and graceful spruce trees grow single needles that roll easily between your fingers. Their broad limbs extend nearly to the ground, and their cones are soft and papery. The blue spruce is Colorado's state tree. Engelman spruce also commonly grow here. Douglas fir, the bullet-shaped conifers, have flat, single needles that can't be rolled in your fingers, their bark is deeply furrowed, and their cones cluster in the highest branches. Douglas fir are genetically different than other fir species, making them "fake fir."

At 8.5 miles, Bedrock Falls appears on the left. A side path leads to photo-taking spots, but don't slip into the chilly water. The main trail continues to Elkhead Pass and access to the Emerald, Iowa, Belford, and Oxford summits. The Continental Divide meanders south of the Pine Creek drainage, so none of these high peaks sits right on the crest.

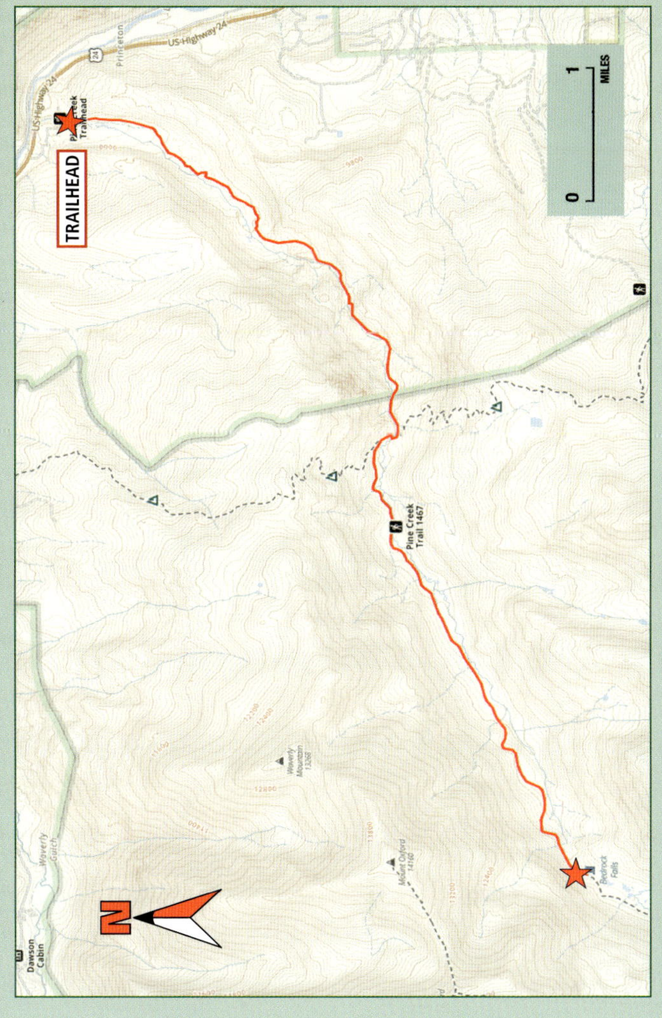
TRAILHEAD
Pine Creek Trailhead
US-Highway 24
Princeton
Pine Creek Trail 1467
Waverly Mountain
Mount Oxford
Bedrock Falls
Waverly Gulch
Dawson Cabin
0
1
MILES
N

6. Emerald and Iowa Peaks

RATING	Difficult
ROUND-TRIP DISTANCE	26.0 miles (from the parking lot); 6.0 miles (from the south base of Elkhead Pass). Backpacking into Pine Creek Valley is recommended for an early start to the following day's climb.
ROUND-TRIP TIME	13 to 17.3 hours (from the parking lot); 3 to 5 hours (from the south base of Elkhead Pass)
STARTING ELEVATION	8,800 feet (parking lot); 11,500 feet (south base of Elkhead Pass)
ENDING ELEVATION	Emerald Peak 13,904 feet; Iowa Peak 13,831 feet
ELEVATION GAIN	For Emerald, 5,100 feet from the parking lot; 2,400 feet from the south base of Elkhead Pass. For Iowa, 5,030 feet from the parking lot; 2,330 feet from the south base of Elkhead Pass. Done together (recommended), 5,590 feet total elevation gain from the parking lot to both summits.
MAPS	Trails Illustrated #129 Buena Vista/ Collegiate Peaks
TRAILHEAD	Pine Creek Trailhead

COMMENT: These beautiful mountains, both among Colorado's 100 highest peaks, offer a pleasant high-altitude hike with only moderate Class 2 talus walking near the summits. They earn a difficult rating because of their altitude and the lengthy approach. Along with Mount Ouray farther south, they are gentle introductions to Colorado's high 13ers that otherwise, on the whole, are harder to summit than the 14ers. Both Iowa and Emerald provide

The key to climbing Iowa and Emerald is first to find the trail leading part way up Elkhead Pass, seen here in the photo's center left. The unmarked route to the 13ers cuts left before the pass.

fabulous views of the Three Apostles and many of the Sawatch Range's 14ers, but without the crowds that swarm those other, slightly higher mountains.

This hike is best done as a backpack into the Pine Creek Valley the first day to allow an early start the next morning to climb the two summits. The traverse from Emerald to Iowa is straightforward, and tackling both summits in one trip eliminates the need to make the 26-mile round trip again. But this enchanted valley may lead you back again and again!

Dogs are allowed on leash. Bird viewing is good: look for ptarmigans. Wildflower viewing is also good, with sky pilot and other alpine species blooming mid-summer after snowmelt. Fall foliage is excellent. There is no fishing. Note that the trail travels miles above timberline, so watch for thunderstorms.

GETTING THERE: Drive US 24 to Chaffee County Road 388. This exit is 38.0 miles north of Salida, 13.7 miles from the Main Street/Cottonwood Pass stoplight in Buena Vista, 22.0 miles south of downtown Leadville, and 4.5 miles south of Granite. Only a small, blue county road sign marks this turn, but CR 388 is north of "The Numbers" river recreation area

Emerald and Iowa Peaks, in the far right, remain spectacular even under smoke-filled skies.

and just south of AVA's Granite Via Ferrata. Exit the highway and drive south on CR 388 for 0.4 miles, then veer left to stay on the main road. Low-clearance passenger cars should park near the sharp curve that appears next. SUVs and high-clearance, two-wheel-drive vehicles can drive another 0.8 mile to the trailhead.

THE HIKE: **For Emerald:** Follow the Pine Creek Trail into the valley. Walk southwest past Bedrock Falls to a junction with both the Elkhead Pass and Silver King Lake Trails. Follow the Elkhead Pass Trail to the right (northwest). The route climbs steeply through the forest, first west and then bending north. This bend is approximately at timberline (just over 12,000 feet) and is roughly 0.9 mile from the previous junction. You may (or may not) see a faint user trail on your left (west),

but if you cross a creek, you missed the unmarked turn. From the side trail's start, hike 0.5 mile on a broad ridge to a bench at 12,500 feet. Pass the pretty alpine tarn (surrounded by summer wildflowers) and keep climbing west for another 0.5 mile to about 13,300 feet. You now are at the base of Emerald's final summit cone, where you start enjoying magnificent views of the Three Apostles. Hike up the northeast ridge 600 feet to the summit.

For Iowa: This summit involves less than another 1.0 mile of hiking and loses/regains about 600 feet each way, making the linkage one of the easiest 13er traverses in Colorado. For Iowa, descend north off Emerald's summit mass for 0.5 mile to the 13,350-foot saddle that connects the two peaks. Clatter up 0.5 mile and 600 feet of moderate talus to Iowa's summit. To descend, return to the saddle, then drop to the bench with the small lake and walk back to the Elkhead Pass Trail.

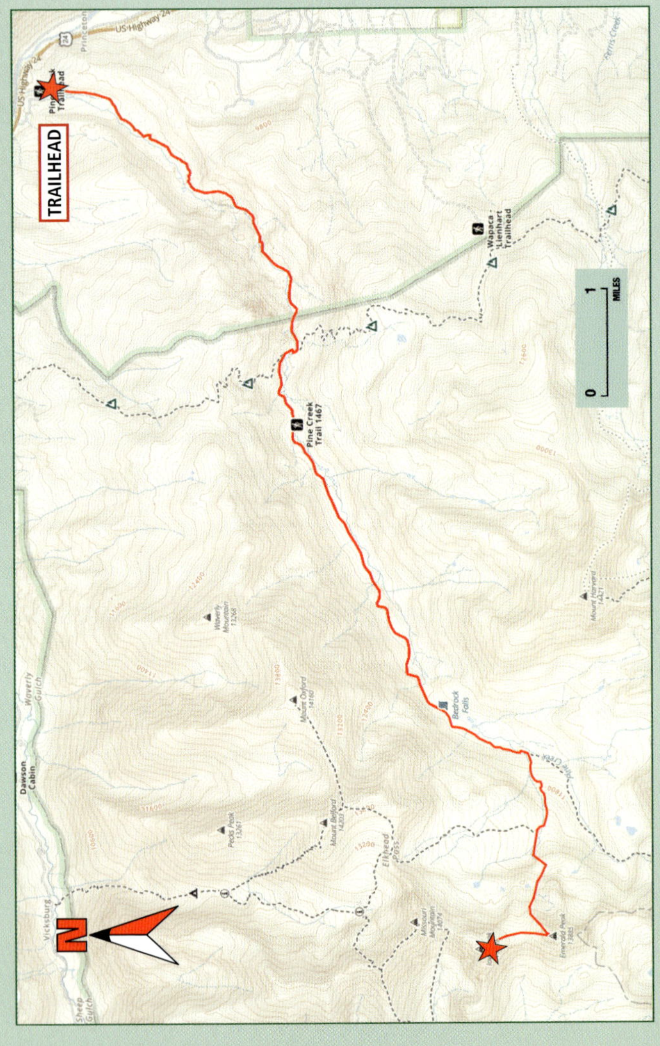
TRAILHEAD
US Highway 24
24
Princeton
Pine Creek Trail 1467
Wapaca-Lienhart Trailhead
Ferris Creek
0
1
MILES
Bedrock Falls
Pine Creek
Waverly Mountain 13,268
Mount Oxford 14,160
Mount Belford 14,203
Pecks Peak 13,261
Elkhead Pass
Missouri Mountain 14,074
Emerald Peak 13,985
Mount Harvard 14,421
Waverly Gulch
Dawson Cabin
Vicksburg
Sheep Gulch
N

7. Mount Belford and Mount Oxford (south approach)

RATING	Difficult
ROUND-TRIP DISTANCE	33.0 miles (from the parking lot); 9.6 miles (from the south base of Elkhead Pass)
ROUND-TRIP TIME	16.5 to 22 hours (from the parking lot); 4.8 to 6.5 hours (from the south base of Elkhead Pass) (backpack recommended)
STARTING ELEVATION	8,800 feet (from the parking lot); 11,500 feet (from the south base of Elkhead Pass)
ENDING ELEVATION	Mount Belford, 14,197 feet; Mount Oxford, 14,153 feet
ELEVATION GAIN	For Belford, 5,397 feet from the parking lot; 2,697 feet from the south base of Elkhead Pass. For Oxford, 5,353 feet from the parking lot; 2,653 feet from the south base of Elkhead Pass. Done together (recommended), 6,400 feet total elevation gain from the parking lot to both summits.
MAPS	Trails Illustrated #129 Buena Vista/ Collegiate Peaks
TRAILHEAD	Pine Creek Trailhead

COMMENT: No matter what route you take, hiking Mounts Belford and Oxford involves steep switchbacks. This trek, though, climbs both 14ers via a less crowded and much prettier approach than the standard, northern route from the Clear Creek drainage. Weather permitting, consider climbing both mountains in the same trip. The saddle between Belford and Oxford is a high altitude walk of 1.5 miles each way with about a 600-foot elevation loss and gain, a mod-

From Elkhead Pass (center), the route up Mount Belford traverses up the weather-exposed ridge to the right.

erate effort worth the extra few hours it takes, unless you prefer to make a second trip up Elkhead Pass to climb these peaks separately. But retreat if the weather threatens to turn ugly because both summits are more than 2,000 feet above the relative safety of timberline.

This hike offers a moderate amount of wildflowers and birds. The fall foliage is excellent. There is no fishing on the peaks. Pay attention for thunderstorms and high winds.

GETTING THERE: Drive US 24 to Chaffee County Road 388. This exit is 38.0 miles north of Salida, 13.7 miles from the Main Street/Cottonwood Pass stoplight in Buena Vista, 22.0 miles south of downtown Leadville, and 4.5 miles south of Granite. Only a small, blue county road sign marks this turn,

Historic Little John's Cabin is a landmark for peakbaggers.

but CR 388 is north of "The Numbers" river recreation area and just south of AVA's Granite Via Ferrata. Exit the highway and drive south on CR 388 for 0.4 miles, then veer left to stay on the main road. Low-clearance passenger cars should park near the sharp curve that appears next. SUVs and high-clearance, two-wheel-drive vehicles can drive another 0.8 mile to the trailhead.

THE HIKE: Follow the Pine Creek Trail to the junction of the Silver King Lake and Elkhead Pass Trails. Take the right fork, the Elkhead Pass Trail. Trudge 2.0 miles up 1,720 feet to the 13,220-foot pass (the state's highest pass); you may grumble on the last few switchbacks. At the pass, catch your breath and look down and north into the Clear Creek drainage. Now, hike 1.0 mile east, then north, on a decent trail that curves across the top of some dramatic cliffs to a Y-shaped junction.

For Oxford, from the Y-shaped intersection, turn northeast on a 1.5-mile path that drops about 500 feet to a wide saddle. Take care walking across the tops of even more dramatic cliffs that plunge down to the Pine Creek drainage. At the top, you may want to sign the summit register. Return to the Y-shaped junction.

For Belford, from the Y-shaped intersection, turn north and hike 0.3 mile, tottering through a rocky area just below the summit. Take pictures and sign the summit register, but take time to eat lunch only if no storms are brewing. Again, return to the Y-shaped junction, thump back to Elkhead Pass, and discover, amazingly, that those steep switchbacks are less strenuous going downhill.

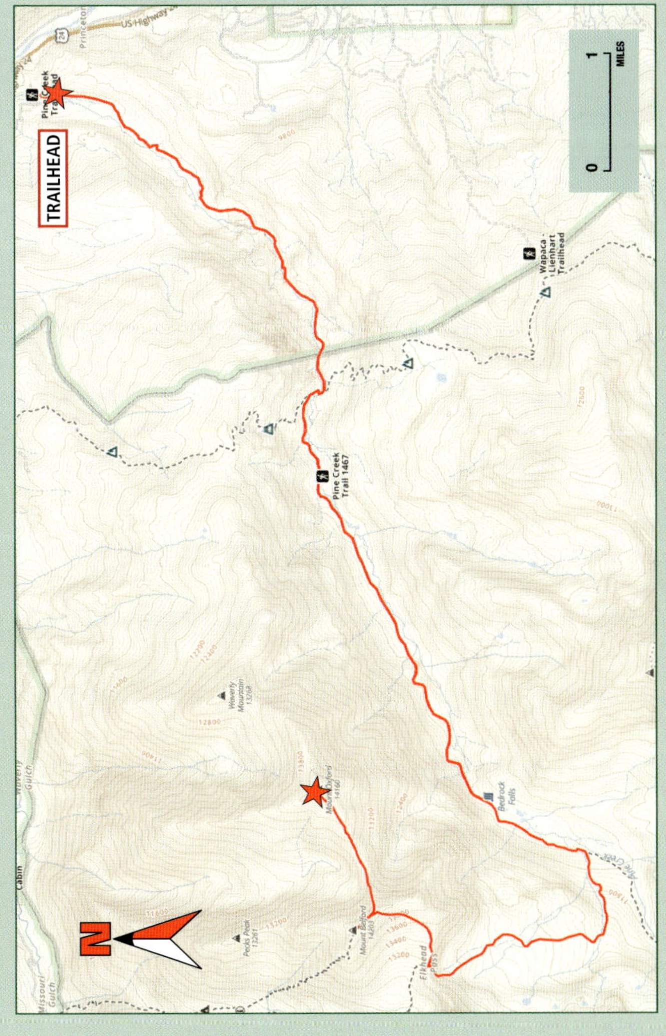
TRAILHEAD
Pine Creek Trail 1467
Wapaca-Lienhart Trailhead
Bedrock Falls
Mount Oxford
Mount Belford
Elkhead Pass
Waverly Mountain
Pecks Peak
MILES

8. Harvard Lakes

RATING	Easy
ROUND-TRIP DISTANCE	6.0 miles
ROUND-TRIP TIME	3 to 4 hours
STARTING ELEVATION	9,400 feet
ENDING ELEVATION	10,300 feet
ELEVATION GAIN	900 feet
MAPS	Trails Illustrated #129 Buena Vista/ Collegiate Peaks
TRAILHEAD	Harvard Lakes Trailhead (North Cottonwood Road access)

COMMENT: This modest hike starts steeply but moderates after the first mile; most grade schoolers can handle the challenge, making this trek popular with families. The well-maintained path leads to two scenic lakes near the base of Mount Columbia. Hikers also get great views of the Upper Arkansas River Valley both on the way up and down. This route follows a few miles of the CT, giving hikers just a taste of the much longer journey.

Dogs are allowed on leash. Bird and wildflower viewing are excellent, as is the fall foliage. The fishing is outstanding. Remain alert for afternoon thunderstorms, especially in the summer, and bug repellant is recommended from spring into early summer.

GETTING THERE: From US Highway 24, drive to the northernmost of Buena Vista's two stoplights and turn west on Chaffee County Road 350/Crossman Avenue. Continue west for 2.0 miles on CR 350. Reach a T-intersection and turn right onto Chaffee County Road 361. Follow CR 361 north for 1.1 miles to a bend, then turn left (southwest) on

"But Mom, I'm part black lab and I really want to swim in Harvard Lakes," whines my dog at the upper lake at the base of Mount Columbia.

County Road 365 (there is a brown sign for Harvard Lakes and the CT). The dirt road gets rough in spots but remains doable for most two-wheel-drive cars with normal clearance (but leave the Lamborghini at home). Please stay on the public right-of-way as the road travels through private land for some distance. After 3.6 miles, reach a small parking area/pullout on the left (south), in the trees and across the road from a north-bound CT marker. If the first lot is full, drive 0.5 mile to the larger Silver Creek Trailhead.

THE HIKE: Start at the CT marker on the *north* side of the road. Follow several switchbacks through classic Chaffee County mid-elevation terrain of brush and junipers, enjoying views of the Upper Arkansas River Valley along the way. Where the trail's grade begins to moderate, the landscape also transforms into a montane ecosystem of pines, spruce, and a smattering of aspen. The first lake is immediately east (right) of the main trail. The second lake is less than 0.25 mile farther, to the left of the trail. Here, the southeast slopes of Mount Columbia loom dramatically above the water. Most people journey to the Harvard Lakes as a day hike, but several campsites nestle in the trees about 100 to 200 feet east of the lakeshore. Good fishing can be found at either lake, but anglers report catching larger trout in the lower lake.

A lone pasqueflower (aka wild crocus or blue tulip) blooms near Harvard Lakes, heralding spring's approach.

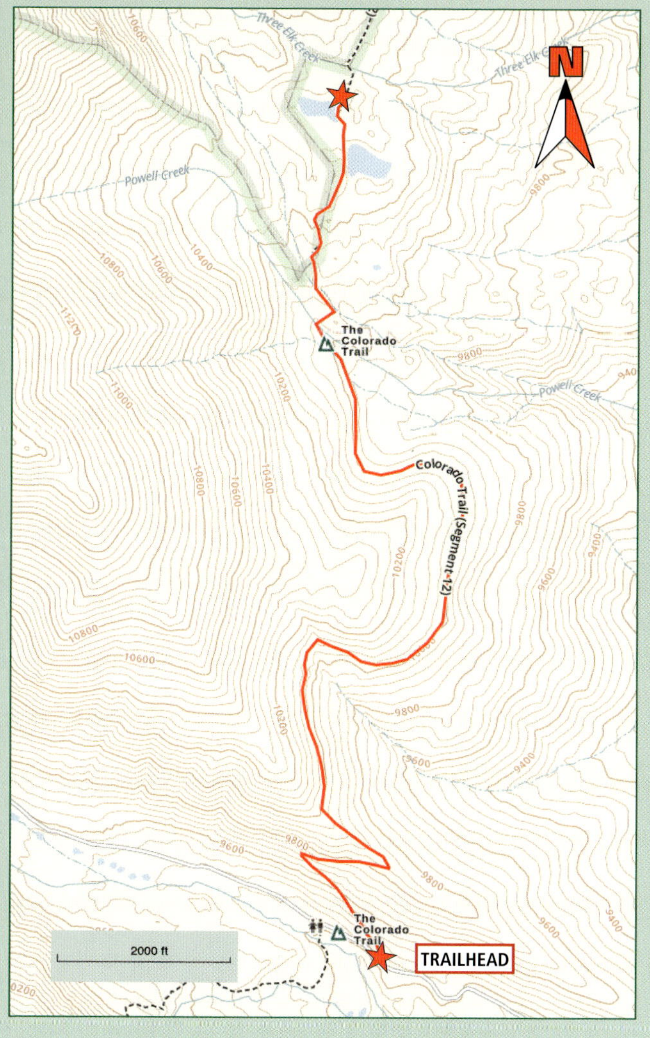
N
Three Elk Creek
Powell Creek
The Colorado Trail
Colorado Trail (Segment 12)
TRAILHEAD
2000 ft

9. The Colorado Trail: Silver Creek to Avalanche Trailhead

RATING	Difficult
ROUND-TRIP DISTANCE	13.0 miles; 6.5 miles one-way with shuttle (recommended)
ROUND-TRIP TIME	6.5 to 8.5 hours (round-trip); 3.25 to 4.7 hours one way
STARTING ELEVATION	9,360 feet (Silver Creek Trailhead); 9,380 feet (Avalanche Trailhead)
HIGHEST ELEVATION	11,900 feet (Mount Yale east shoulder)
ELEVATION GAIN	From Silver Creek, 2,540 feet; from Avalanche Trailhead, 2,520 feet
MAPS	Trails Illustrated #129 Buena Vista/ Collegiate Peaks
TRAILHEAD	Silver Creek Trailhead (North Cottonwood Road access)

COMMENT: This trail provides great views, a variety of ecosystems, and the potential for wildflowers, wildlife, and bird-watching. But it's steep and strenuous from either direction. The route is part of the CT's Segment 13, which I found more interesting than the official segment's southern stretch. This hike is best accomplished as a one-way trek using a car shuttle with a vehicle at each trailhead. Most people should start at Silver Creek and hike south to Avalanche Gulch, unless they have such bad knees that going downhill is painful, in which case they might not want to attempt this trail anyway.

The wildflowers are excellent here in early summer as is the fall foliage. Bird viewing opportunities are good. There is no fishing. Stay alert for thunderstorms, high winds, and spring snowdrifts.

Section 13 of the Colorado Trail travels the steep slopes on Mount Yale's eastern shoulder.

GETTING THERE:

For the hike's northern start at the Silver Creek Trailhead: From US Highway 24, drive to the northernmost of Buena Vista's two stoplights and turn west on Chaffee County Road 350/Crossman Avenue. Continue west for 2.0 miles on CR 350. Reach a T-intersection and turn right onto Chaffee County Road 361. Follow CR 361 north for 1.1 miles to a bend, then turn left (southwest) on County Road 365 (there is a brown sign for Harvard Lakes and the CT). The dirt road gets rough in spots but remains doable for most two-wheel-drive cars with normal clearance (but leave the Lamborghini at home). Please stay on the public right-of-way as the road travels through private land for some distance. After 4.1 miles, reach the Silver Creek Trailhead, which has pit toilets.

For the Avalanche Trailhead at the hike's southern end: Find the southernmost of Buena Vista's two stoplights off

The CT's southbound descent toward the Avalanche Gulch Trailhead includes views of Rainbow Lake.

US Highway 24. Turn west onto Main Street/Cottonwood Pass Road, which becomes Chaffee County Road 306 west of town. The road is paved the whole way. Follow CR 306 for 9.3 miles to a sign that says "Avalanche Trailhead" and points right (north). Turn into the huge lot (which fills on summer weekends) and park. This trailhead also has pit toilets.

THE HIKE: From the Silver Creek Trailhead, head south on the CT, cross North Cottonwood Creek on a solid wooden bridge, and walk into a soothing spruce-fir forest. Listen for the many bird species. About 2.0 miles from the trailhead, the path begins paralleling Silver Creek. Cross the stream at 2.5 miles; filter water and fill your bottles here if need be as the next water is nearly 4.0 miles south. Start climbing; from this direction the angle begins moderately. The trail then encounters some switchbacks just below Mount Yale's east shoulder. (Some people climb Yale this way, but an easier route to the summit is described later in this guide.) The CT sneaks between two lumps on the big ridge, but the high point here still offers great views. Now the trail turns almost straight south, plunging into a ravine and losing about 1,000 feet in roughly 1.0 mile. Aren't you glad you were warned to not hike up that grueling plumbline? (I'll take chocolate as a thank you gift.) The ravine holds moisture, so in early summer it fills with wildflowers. The slope angle moderates as the forest opens up, offering more views. The aspen groves here turn magnificent hues of gold and red in autumn. About 0.5 mile from your shuttle car, notice the gem-like Rainbow Lake to the southeast. Hopefully, extra bottles of clean water await in your car because after this trek, you may find that the precious liquid tastes better than the finest wine.

The CT meanders near small mountain creeks along Section 13's northern stretch.

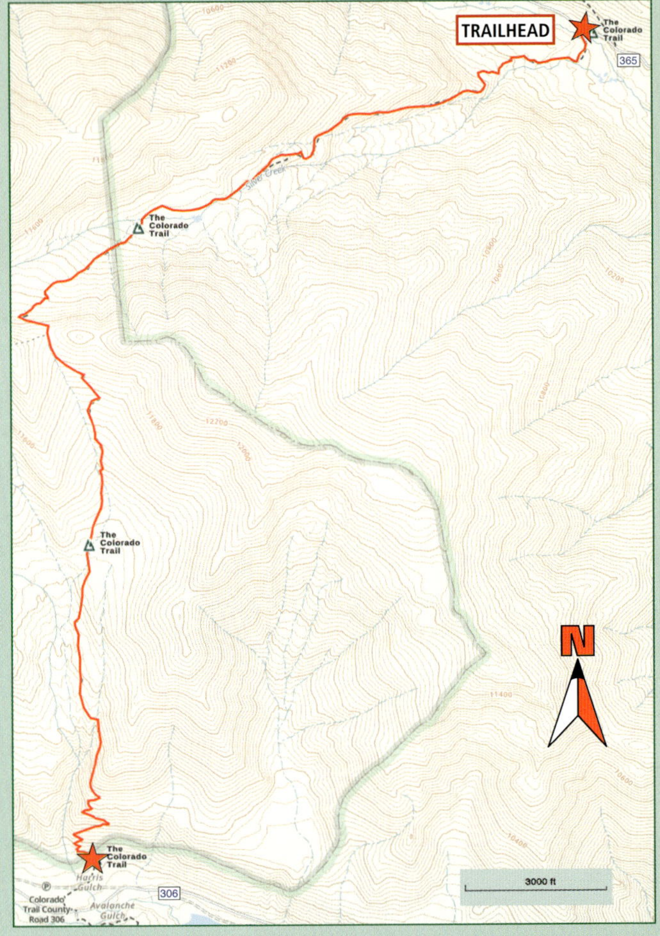
TRAILHEAD
The Colorado Trail
365
Silver Creek
The Colorado Trail
The Colorado Trail
N
The Colorado Trail
Harris Gulch
306
Colorado Trail County Road 306
Avalanche Gulch
3000 ft

10. Whipple Trail

RATING	Easy
ROUND-TRIP DISTANCE	1.4 miles to 3.3 miles (short loops); longer variations are possible
ROUND-TRIP TIME	1 hour to 3.5 hours
STARTING ELEVATION	7,900 feet
HIGHEST ELEVATION	8,200 feet
ELEVATION GAIN	300 feet
MAPS	Buena Vista town map; Trails Illustrated #129 Buena Vista/ Collegiate Peaks
TRAILHEAD	Whipple Trail / Midland Hill Bridge

COMMENT: This close-to-town trail is perfect for days when storms strafe the high country or your legs need a rest. Several other trails intersect it, creating many longer variations that let you make the trek as short and easy, or as long and heart-pumping, as you like. The hike as described here meanders through pinyon pine, scrub brush, and granitic outcrops, while offering sweeping views of the Sawatch Range to the west, the Arkansas River directly below the path, and the town of Buena Vista. The trail is named for Barbara Whipple, a longtime Buena Vista resident, artist, art gallery owner, and avid hiker.

Dogs are allowed on leash. Good bird viewing is available. Wildflower viewing is fair, but the fall foliage is excellent. The fishing is also excellent, given the Gold Medal Water in the Arkansas River below the trail. Be on the lookout for mountain bikers.

GETTING THERE: Two good foot/bicycle bridges cross the Arkansas River, so you can hike the loops from either direction. For the north trailhead, find East Main Street in downtown

North access to the Whipple Trail crosses the Arkansas River on a solid footbridge.

Buena Vista and drive the paved road east to a T-intersection near the river. Turn north into a large, free public parking area with drinking fountains, restrooms, and trash and recycle bins. For the south trailhead, from downtown Buena Vista drive east on Riverpark Road until the street dead-ends near the river. Free public parking is just north of the street. Note that South Main Street connects East Main and Riverpark Road, which parallels the river.

THE HIKE: This description follows the north-to-south route. From the parking area, cross the Arkansas River on an excellent foot/bicycle bridge, turn right, and walk 0.1 mile to an intersection. At this intersection, turn left for the Whipple shortcut (because very few bikes use it) and hike 0.15 mile up a short, sandy hill. At the top of the small hill, reach a second intersection and take the right fork. Climb slightly for 0.2 mile along rolling terrain, getting great views of the

Sawatch, the river, and downtown Buena Vista. Reach a third junction and decide whether to continue on the shortest route or the longer hikes. For the shortest loop, at this third trail intersection, turn right and head downhill; this trail segment soon joins a short piece of the Midland Gravel bike route and follows approximately 0.5 mile back to the north parking area. For a moderately longer loop, follow the short loop to the third intersection, but don't turn right. Instead, go straight (south) for 0.4 mile on part of the Bridge-to-Bridge path, which at first stays fairly level, then zigzags downhill and west. Reach a level, open area and walk west a few hundred yards. Make sure to respect the surrounding private property here. Cross the river on an excellent new bridge. Read two signs on the Ark's west side: One placard

BV's Riverwalk on the Ark's western banks lets hikers watch kayakers play in the rapids.

Whipple Trail travels through a drier ecosystem than other BV area treks, but it's a good hike when storms rake the higher terrain to the west.

offers a serious warning about the dangerous river rapids. The other is a hilarious ode to hikers and their dogs. Follow the Buena Vista Riverwalk Trail north 0.7 mile to the car, passing several businesses where hikers can get coffee or beer. Several other treks are possible from both trailheads, either as loop hikes or by using a car shuttle. Check the maps at the trailheads if you don't have a copy.

Note: The Buena Vista Riverwalk on the Ark's western bank is wheelchair accessible. The surface varies from tightly packed sand to pavement. This path provides an opportunity to share the river's beauty and views of the hillsides and riparian ecosystems with elderly or disabled friends and family members.

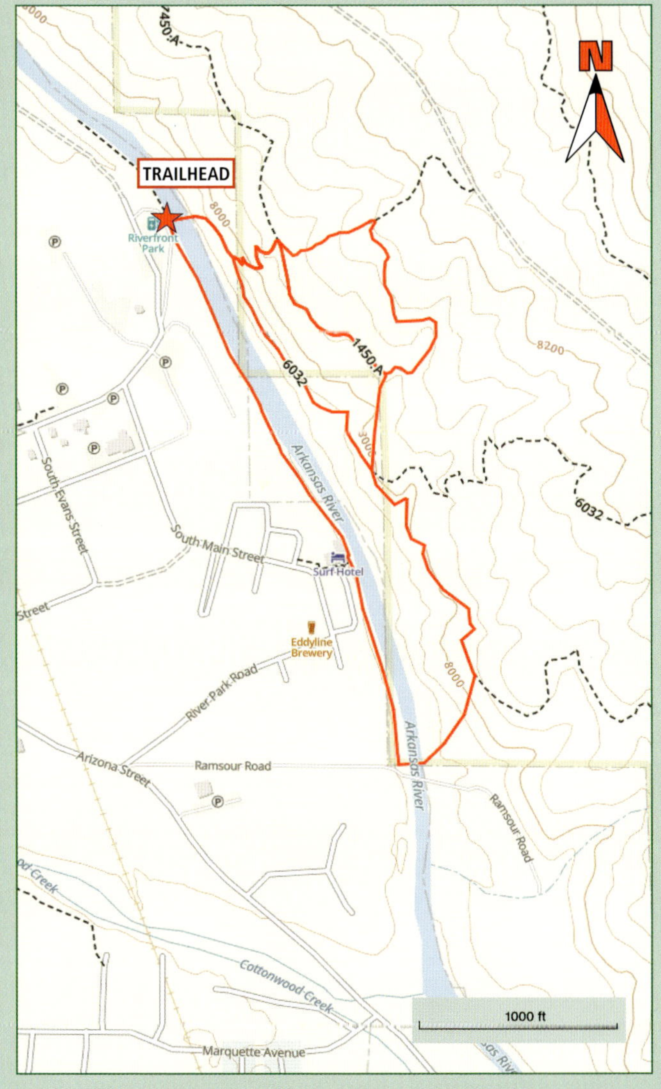
N
TRAILHEAD
Riverfront Park
7450.A
8000
1450.A
6032
8200
Arkansas River
South Evans Street
South Main Street
Surf Hotel
Eddyline Brewery
River Park Road
Arizona Street
Ramsour Road
Cottonwood Creek
Marquette Avenue
1000 ft

11. Mount Yale

RATING	Difficult; Class 2 and rocky above timberline
ROUND-TRIP DISTANCE	9.6 miles
ROUND-TRIP TIME	8 to 12 hours
STARTING ELEVATION	9,900 feet
ENDING ELEVATION	14,196 feet
ELEVATION GAIN	4,300 feet
MAPS	Trails Illustrated #129 Buena Vista/ Collegiate Peaks
TRAILHEAD	Denny Creek Trailhead

COMMENT: This scenic but steep hike follows a well-built trail through old-growth forest, mostly along a tumbling creek flanked by wildflowers. The Forest Service and the Colorado Fourteeners Initiative (CFI) want hikers to use this main trail (Denny Creek) because they had to close other popular routes due to overuse and severe erosion. CFI reworked the Denny Creek route in 2008–2011 to reduce erosion and protect wildlife habitat and the creek's water quality. Yale is the easiest 14er in the Buena Vista/Salida area and is popular with families, but it's *not* a beginner hike. The trail is relentlessly steep and involves several small stream crossings, and above timberline, you labor through a jumble of boulders before reaching the long, weather-exposed summit ridge. Consider those factors when deciding what's right for your family. Note that many online sources significantly understate the distance, which is 9.6 miles round-trip.

Dogs are allowed on leash. Bird, wildflower, and fall foliage viewing are all excellent. There is no fishing. Remain alert for thunderstorms, and there is avalanche hazard from winter to late spring.

After it emerges from the boulders, the trail up Mount Yale cuts across the face of the hump (on the left in this photo), then bends north around the hump toward the ridge (leading left to right in the photo). The true summit is along the ridge, just out of view here.

GETTING THERE: From the southernmost of Buena Vista's two stoplights, turn west on Main Street, which is also signed as Cottonwood Pass/County Road 306. It's paved the entire distance so is passable to passenger cars from spring to fall. Drive 12.0 miles to a sign that says Mount Yale; turn right (north) here and find a large parking area with a pit toilet. Arrive early in the morning because the lot serves several trails and fills quickly with cars, particularly in summer. Overflow parking can be found a mile east at the Avalanche Trailhead.

THE HIKE: Walk north from the lot on a well-signed trail. After about 1.0 mile, cross Denny Creek on a decent log bridge, then hop another seasonal brook a short distance later. At about 1.3 miles from the car, reach a junction with the Hartenstein Lake hike (also described in this book). Take the right fork at the sign pointing to Mount Yale. About 2.25 miles from the car, balance on small logs across yet another creek. Continue on the obvious but steep trail, intermittently grunting up stony steps (some so tall that they may make short people say bad words). Approximately 3.4 miles into

Happy hikers stay on the trail while descending from their successful Mount Yale summit.

the hike, reach alpine tundra at roughly 12,000 feet. Don't underestimate the final 1.4 miles and 2,196 feet of upward trek: the big hill you see from this point is just Yale's west shoulder, not its summit. Follow rock cairns through the boulder field. After the boulders, the route turns right and eventually ascends and traverses below Yale's shoulder. Reach a saddle at 13,900 feet and catch your breath. The last 300 feet of talus is doable Class 2 but at this altitude demands tenacity. Enjoy the summit vista but don't tarry too long. Take your time going down; the steep descent may further tire your already weary muscles.

A marmot warns its kin that a peakbagger and a dog are coming up the boulder field on Mount Yale.

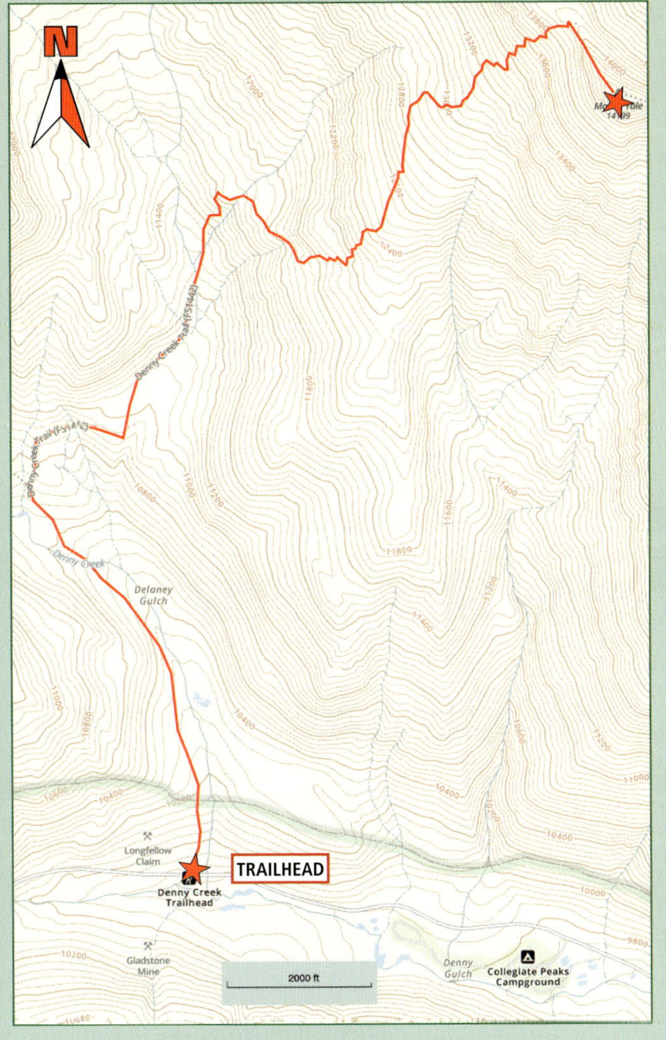
N
Denny Creek Trail (FS1442)
Denny Creek Trail (FS1442)
Denny Creek
Delaney Gulch
Longfellow Claim
TRAILHEAD
Denny Creek Trailhead
Gladstone Mine
2000 ft
Denny Gulch
Collegiate Peaks Campground

12. Hartenstein Lake

RATING	Moderate
ROUND-TRIP DISTANCE	5.8 miles
ROUND-TRIP TIME	3 to 5 hours
STARTING ELEVATION	9,880 feet
HIGHEST ELEVATION	11,480 feet
ELEVATION GAIN	1,600 feet
MAPS	Trails Illustrated #129 Buena Vista/ Collegiate Peaks
TRAILHEAD	Denny Creek Trailhead

COMMENT: This hike starts steeply but moderates before reaching the lake, cocooned at the base of the Continental Divide. Along the way, the trail travels through spruce-fir forest; hillsides offering views across the Cottonwood Creek drainage; a new-growth aspen forest; and past a high-altitude wetland. Once at the main lake, notice how nature's power recently remade the landscape; for example, an avalanche in winter 2018–19 sent large trees crashing into the lake's western edge. The trail merits a moderate rating only because the first 2.0 miles work your legs, but the angle relents during the last mile before the lake, making for a pleasant half-day stroll. In winter, this trail is also popular for snowshoeing, but always check avalanche conditions.

Dogs on leash are allowed. Bird viewing is excellent. Wildflower viewing is excellent, especially during early summer. The fall foliage is also excellent. The fishing is good. Stay alert for thunderstorms, particularly by the lake and in other open areas. There is avalanche hazard from late fall to early spring.

GETTING THERE: From the southernmost of Buena Vista's two stoplights, turn west on Main Street, which is also signed

Hartenstein Lake gets fewer visitors than other local lakes. Logs float on the far shore, brought down by an avalanche in winter 2018–2019.

as Cottonwood Pass/County Road 306. It's paved the entire distance so is passable to passenger cars from spring to fall. Drive 12.0 miles to a sign that says Mount Yale; turn right (north) here and find a large parking area with a pit toilet. Arrive early in the morning because the lot serves several trails and fills quickly with cars, particularly in summer. Overflow parking can be found a mile east at the Avalanche Trailhead. Hartenstein Lake shares the parking lot and trailhead with Mount Yale.

In spring and early summer, the Hartenstein Lake Trail offers nice wildflower viewing.

The 2018–2019 avalanche snapped mature conifers near their base. The trekking poles provide scale.

THE HIKE: Hike south and uphill on the same trail that leads to Mount Yale, parallel to Denny Creek. In 1.3 miles at a sign, go left at a trail fork. (The right fork heads up Yale.) Contour up and along an open hillside, getting views across the valley. Cross a small side stream. About 0.7 mile from the Yale junction, again bear left at the next signed intersection with the Browns Pass Trail. Cross Browns Creek on small logs or rocks. In the last mile, wander into an aspen forest with relatively young trees that barely reach above head-height. This part of the path makes for an extraordinary autumn walk. Moose and other wildlife often browse among the ponds and riparian habitat below the trail. The path opens into a wide bowl surrounded by mountains just as the trail reaches the lake. Several tree stumps and fallen logs make good picnic spots. Anglers should look for small paths leading to the water's edge, but debris from the 2018–19 avalanche buried part of the old trail and made walking around the entire lake impossible.

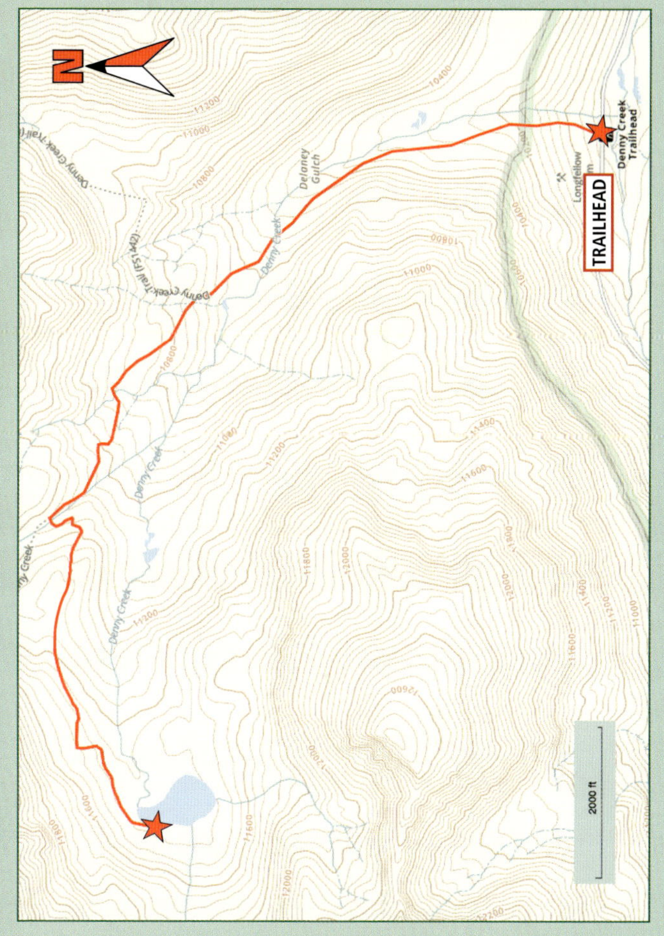
TRAILHEAD
Denny Creek Trailhead
Longfellow
Delaney Gulch
Denny Creek
Denny Creek Trail (FS1442)
2000 ft

13. Ptarmigan Lake

RATING	Moderate
ROUND-TRIP DISTANCE	6.8 miles
ROUND-TRIP TIME	3.4 to 5.5 hours
STARTING ELEVATION	10,680 feet
ENDING ELEVATION	12,300 feet
ELEVATION GAIN	1,620 feet
MAPS	Trails Illustrated #129 Buena Vista/ Collegiate Peaks
TRAILHEAD	Ptarmigan Lake Trailhead (Cottonwood Pass Road access)

COMMENT: Dramatic views of Mount Yale and the surrounding high 13ers await hikers who push all the way to the Ptarmigan Lake's shores. Many people don't quite complete the full trek, however, preferring to stop at the lovely high-altitude ponds just below timberline, where trunks of fallen trees provide perfect picnic perches. Several excellent campsites hide amid the conifers here, too. Just a bit farther up, the meadows erupt in wildflowers in late spring and early summer. The entire trail offers great views and bird-watching, but don't expect solitude on a summer weekend, given that the trailhead is right next to the popular, paved Cottonwood Pass Road and scenic drive.

Dogs are allowed on leash. The bird, wildflower, and fall foliage viewing are excellent. The fishing is exceptional. Watch out for moose and thunderstorms.

GETTING THERE: From the southernmost of Buena Vista's two stoplights, turn west on Main Street, which is also signed as Cottonwood Pass/County Road 306. It's paved the entire distance so is passable to passenger cars from spring to fall. Drive 14.5 miles to a sign that says Ptarmigan Lake. Note

Ptarmigan Lake is a popular destination for anglers and families, but its high-altitude location doesn't offer much shelter from the sun or the wind.

that the turn is on the left (south) side of the road, so watch for oncoming traffic. The parking lot has two parts; the upper lot has the pit toilet. The trail starts downhill from the pit toilet on the south side of the paved, upper parking area. Some people mistake the unmaintained fishing access path west of the outhouse for the main trail; if you don't soon encounter an obvious footbridge, you're on the wrong route.

THE HIKE: Head south and cross Cottonwood Creek on a great footbridge. The trail bends to the left and begins a long switchback through the spruce-fir forest. About 0.5 mile from the creek, start stepping carefully along a wide rockslide, where the trail remains remarkably level and easy to follow, thanks to careful tending by local volunteers and Forest Service professionals. Notice flecks of mica—"fool's gold"—embedded in the boulders along the way. The path returns primarily to dirt at about 1.0 mile. About 1.4 miles from the car, the route crosses an old road. Continue uphill on the hiking path. Approximately 2.0 miles from the trailhead, enter the land of meadows and small lakes. Many people stop at the largest of these scenic tarns, preferring not to push up the final 1.2 miles to the true Ptarmigan

The view just below Ptarmigan Lake looks back toward the Cottonwood Pass Road and Mount Yale area.

Lake. Hikers who persevere will be rewarded with ever more dramatic views of the Sawatch Range's high peaks, including Mount Yale.

Just below the final ridge, hop across the tiny brook flowing from Ptarmigan Spring. Start looking for the eponymous birds, camouflaged in brown during summer and hidden by white plumage in wintertime. Past the ridge, expect to see anglers trying their luck at the lake. Near the lake, the old shrubs deformed by wicked weather don't offer shade or wind protection, so bring sun hats with chin straps or cap keepers. A trail circumnavigates the lake, while another path leads to a four-wheel-drive road on the south side. The ruggedness of the steep dirt road, followed by a too-short hike, are reasons that most people get to the lake via this hike rather than the rough dirt road to the south.

Just below timberline, Ptarmigan Lake hikers find places to picnic near subalpine ponds.

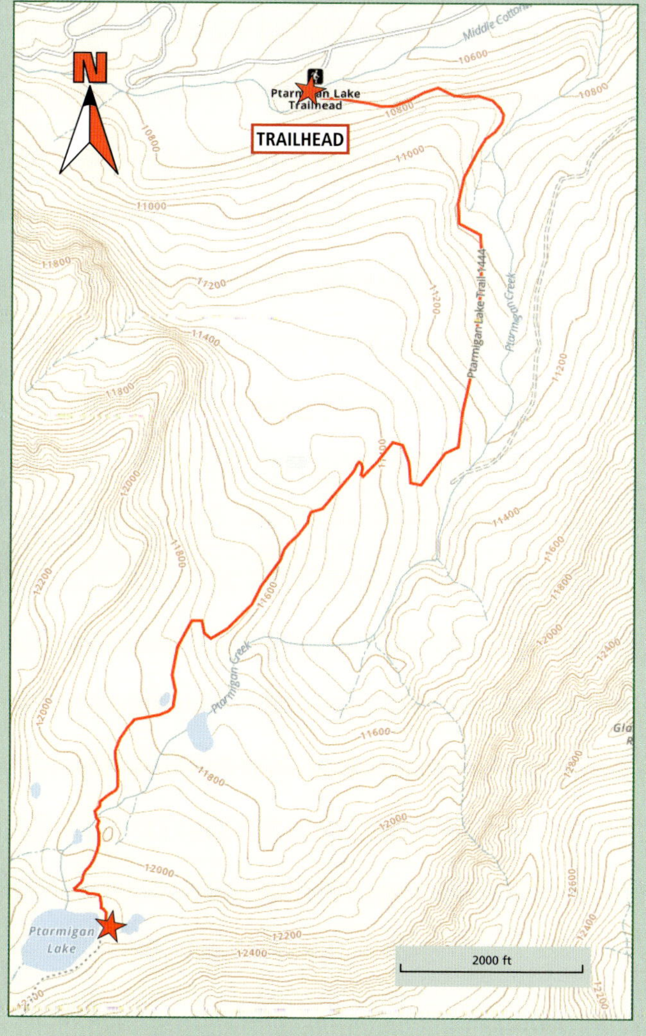
N
Ptarmigan Lake Trailhead
TRAILHEAD
Middle Cottonwood
Ptarmigan Lake Trail 1444
Ptarmigan Creek
Ptarmigan Creek
Ptarmigan Lake
2000 ft

14. Mount Princeton

RATING	Difficult; Class 2
ROUND-TRIP DISTANCE	13.6 miles (from the lower passenger car lot); 6.8 miles (from the upper four-wheel-drive parking)
ROUND-TRIP TIME	7 to 14 hours; an early start is recommended
STARTING ELEVATION	8,800 feet (lower two-wheel-drive parking); 10,880 feet (upper four-wheel-drive lot)
ENDING ELEVATION	14,197
ELEVATION GAIN	5,400 feet from the two-wheel-drive (passenger car) parking at the Young Life Center; 3,320 feet from the upper four-wheel-drive parking area near the radio towers.
MAPS	Trails Illustrated #130 Salida/ St. Elmo/Mount Shavano
TRAILHEAD	Chaffee County Road 162 access

COMMENT: Mount Princeton towers above the Arkansas River Valley; it's the most prominent peak seen from Trout Creek Pass. Views from its summit are equally regal. Although the mountain is an obvious goal for hikers, it's not a beginner's peak because of its elevation gain and long exposure above timberline. It is a good idea to first hike Mount Yale and Mount Huron before attempting Princeton. The route involves a long approach on a boulder-filled road that's passable only to high-clearance/high-powered SUVs and requires "technical" four-wheel-driving skills. Unless you want to put your mechanic's kids through college, leave your two-wheel-drive cars at the Young Life Center parking area, and stash even four-wheel-drive vehicles at or just beyond the radio towers.

The hike up Mount Princeton stays above timberline for many miles.

Dogs are allowed, and leashes are recommended, given the traffic. Bird viewing is fair; look for raptors over the open areas. Wildflowers are fair in early summer. Fall foliage is also fair. There is no fishing. This route is exposed to weather, so watch for thunderstorms. Pay attention on the rocky trail and be mindful of symptoms resulting from the long time at high altitude. Winter avalanches are common on the upper slopes.

GETTING THERE: The simplest of several ways to get to the trailhead is, from US 285, turn west on Chaffee County Road 162 at a sign that says "Mount Princeton Resort/St. Elmo." This junction is 9.8 miles south of Buena Vista and 19.5 miles north of Poncha Springs. Follow CR 162 for about 4.4 miles, then turn right (north) on Chaffee County Road 321. Follow a long curve to a T-intersection; turn left here onto Chaffee County Road 322 and follow it 1.0 mile, ignoring a side road leading downhill. Reach the privately owned Young Life Center, which offers pit toilets for hikers. Passenger cars should stop here. High-clearance SUVs can continue on the

The turn off the four-wheel-drive road to the Mount Princeton trail isn't marked, so look for the small conifer next to the stone steps.

These flowers, called Old Man of the Mountain, manage to survive harsh alpine winters on Mount Princeton's eastern side.

rough road for 1.1. miles to the radio towers, passing a CT junction on the way. Limited parking and dry camping spots exist at and just beyond the towers along the road.

THE HIKE: Walk the road either from the Young Life Center or the radio towers. Trudge around several stony switchbacks. At about 11,800 feet, after a tight switchback and before a long straightaway, look on the right (north) side of the road for a lone conifer next to a massive rock cairn and some stone steps: That's where the Mount Princeton summit trail exits the road. The dirt hiking path will do your soles good after enduring the rocky four-wheel-drive route. The trail starts heading slightly northwest, then veers southwest, crosses a large open basin, and contours up a long, stony slope. This piece of trail is surprisingly time-consuming. Reach Princeton's extensive southeast shoulder at about 13,500 feet. Turn north and plod up the final rocky 600 feet to the summit. Enjoy the view before heading down the same route.

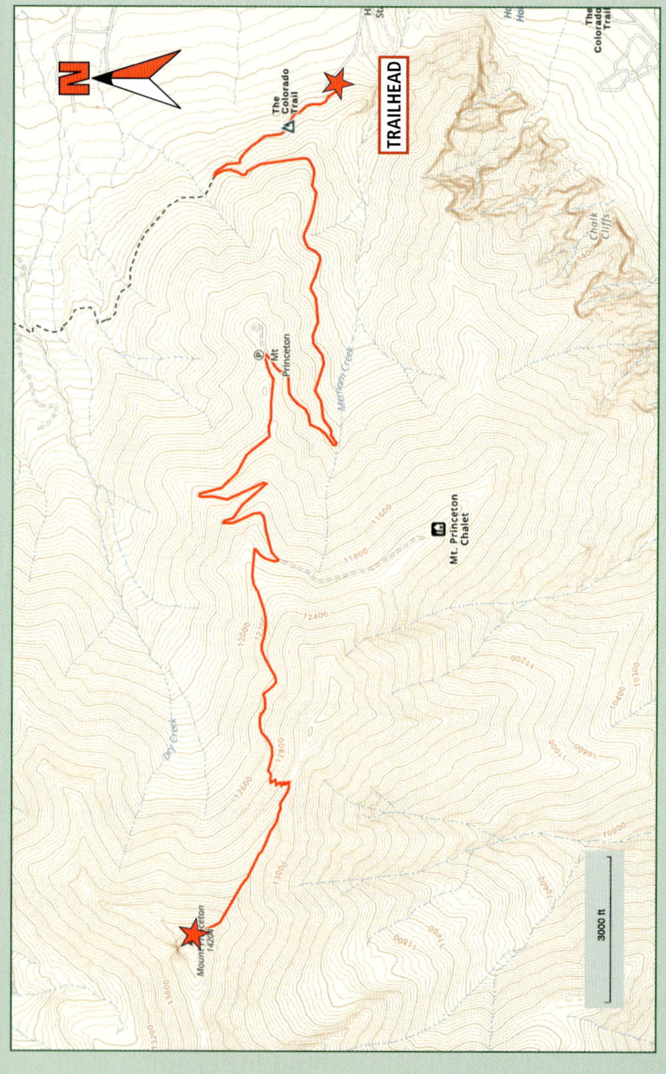
N
TRAILHEAD
The Colorado Trail
Mt Princeton
Merriam Creek
Mt. Princeton Chalet
Chalk Cliffs
Dry Creek
11600
11800
12400
12000
12800
12600
13000
13600
3000 ft

15. Narrow Gauge Trail

RATING	Easy
ROUND-TRIP DISTANCE	3.0 miles
ROUND-TRIP TIME	1.5 to 3 hours
STARTING ELEVATION	8,920 feet
ENDING ELEVATION	8,920 feet
ELEVATION GAIN	50 feet (gain/loss both ways)
MAPS	Trails Illustrated #130 Salida/ St. Elmo/Mount Shavano
TRAILHEAD	Chalk Creek Trailhead

COMMENT: This path is a short segment of a much longer route used in the late nineteenth century by the narrow-gauge railroad. Although the trail is not wheelchair accessible, it's suitable for families with young children and for grown-ups who prefer a gentle hike. Hikers enjoy stunning views of the Chalk Cliffs, the massive bulk of Mount Princeton's south side, and views of Wrights Lake and State Wildlife area. Private land surrounds the eastern trailhead, so stay on the access road and public right-of-way. Use the eastern trailhead and do an easy round-trip, because the western end drops to County Road 162 near Cascade Falls, where speeding SUVs and lumbering RVs present real risks when you're parking or walking along the paved road.

Dogs are allowed if leashed. Bird viewing is fair; you may spy raptors in the cliffs across the road. Wildflower viewing is fair, but fall foliage is excellent. There is fishing below the trail in the state wildlife area or along Chalk Creek. Keep an eye out for mountain bikers.

GETTING THERE: Follow the directions from US 285 to the turn for Mount Princeton onto Chaffee County Road 162. Drive

The gentle Narrow Gauge Trail offers views of Wrights Lake State Wildlife Area, the Chalk Cliffs, and Mount Princeton's eastern shoulder.

west on CR 162 for 10.0 miles to the junction with County Road 290; turn left onto CR 290. Drive slowly through the residential area for about 1.2 miles to the road's terminus, the parking lot, and the suggested eastern trailhead. For the western trailhead, which is *not* recommended, stay on CR 162 for another 3.0 miles to the parking area for Cascade Falls on the highway's north (right) side. The obscure Narrow Gauge Trailhead is on the other (south) side of the

The Chalk Cliffs can spontaneously shed massive amounts of rock and dirt, so I don't recommend hiking at their base. Enjoy the view from across the creek along the Narrow Gauge Trail.

twisting, busy road, about 100 yards west of the parking area and almost directly above the cascades. Use caution walking along and crossing the road because of wide RVs and speeding vehicles.

THE HIKE: Enjoy reading the historical sign at the trailhead, then saunter along the dirt path that's usually wide enough to let a hiker and mountain biker pass each other easily. Step around the occasional chunks of light-colored granite. These trailside rocks are different than those you see on the crags to the north, across the river and highway. The Chalk Cliffs are mostly a soft, clay-like substance called

Informational signs at both ends of the Narrow Gauge Trail describe local history.

kaolinite, which forms when hot water percolates through quartz. (And of course, quartz is a key component of granite.) Marvel at Mount Princeton's corrugated, towering southern flank. Look down on aspens and Chalk Creek's thriving riparian ecosystem. Near the trail's midpoint, walk up and down a rocky step that barely gains 10 feet and lasts less than 20 yards. Good wooden bridges cross two side streams, the first at about 0.25 mile from the eastern trailhead and the second near the western trailhead. Occasional aspens and stone blocks provide shade and places to sit for impromptu picnics. Return to the eastern trailhead, where you showed good judgment by heeding the author's advice to make the hike a round-trip journey.

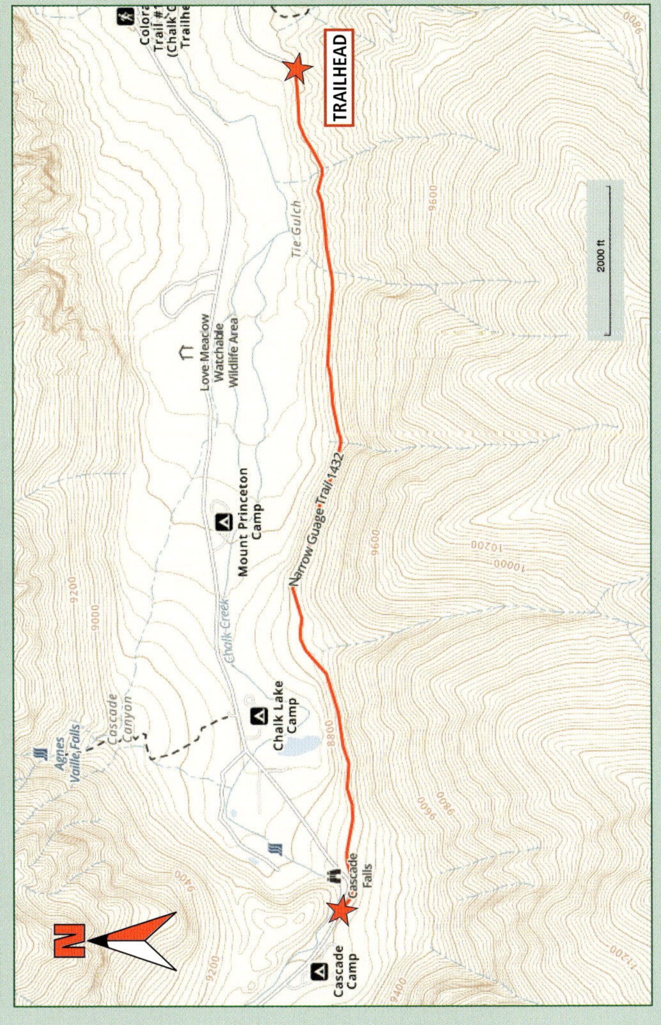
TRAILHEAD
Tie Gulch
9600
2000 ft
Love Meadow Watchable Wildlife Area
Mount Princeton Camp
Narrow Guage Trail 1432
10200
10000
9200
9000
Chalk Creek
Cascade Canyon
Chalk Lake Camp
8800
Agnes Vaille Falls
9800
Cascade Falls
9400
N
Cascade Camp
11200

16. Browns Falls and Lake

RATING	Easy (falls) to moderate (lake)
ROUND-TRIP DISTANCE	6.0 miles (to the falls); 12.0 miles (to the lake)
ROUND-TRIP TIME	6 to 8 hours (full hike); 1.5 to 4 hours (partial hike)
STARTING ELEVATION	8,900 feet
ENDING ELEVATION	11,320 (at the lake); 9,870 feet (at the falls)
ELEVATION GAIN	2,400 (to the lake); 970 feet (to the falls)
MAPS	Trails Illustrated #130 Salida/ St. Elmo
TRAILHEAD	Browns Creek Trailhead

COMMENT: This popular trail meanders through conifers and aspens on its way to a scenic waterfall, then climbs steadily to an alpine lake that's flanked by two 13ers. On the way, the path crosses streams and passes through mature pine and spruce forests that are home to songbirds and deer, elk, moose, and other wildlife. The easy walk to the falls makes a nice day hike. The trek past the falls to the lake climbs steadily, making it appropriate for a backpack and earning the full journey a moderate rating. The path also intersects with the CT and the Wagon Loop Trail, described elsewhere in this book. A 2019 flood damaged the dam that held the lake so the water level fell, but the place retains its charm.

Dogs are allowed, and a leash is recommended. Bird viewing is good. Wildflower viewing is good, too, especially near the lake. Fall foliage is excellent. Fishing is good, in both the creek and lake. Be on the lookout for moose and mountain bikers.

A popular day hike leads to Browns Creek Falls. To reach the cascade hikers must exit Browns Lake Trail and ascend a short, rocky access path.

GETTING THERE: From US 285, turn west onto Chaffee County Road 270, which soon turns to dirt but remains passable to passenger cars. This turn is 15.4 miles north of the US 285/ US 50 intersection near Poncha Springs, 2.5 miles south of the junction of US 285 and US 24, and 11.3 miles south of Buena Vista. Once on CR 270, drive west 1.5 miles to a four-way intersection. Go straight west on Forest Service Road 272 (do not turn right to stay on CR 270). Follow Forest Service Road 272 for 2.0 miles, then turn left. Drive about 1.5 miles to a large trailhead and a pit toilet. There is no potable water here.

Take care maneuvering around large boulders to get close the falls, where the air feels wonderfully cool on a hot summer's day.

THE HIKE: The trail starts by ascending steadily but moderately through aspen and ponderosa pine stands populated by flickers, woodpeckers, and numerous songbirds. At 1.4 miles, reach an intersection with the Little Browns Creek Trail and the CT; turn left onto the southbound CT. At 1.6 miles, cross a creek on a good bridge. A few hundred yards later, reach another junction and turn right (west) toward Browns Lake. At 1.7 miles, cross another stream either on logs or by hopping on rocks. Walk through a meadow where you may see moose or other large mammals grazing. At 2.6 miles, the trail reaches the horse ford across Browns Creek; hikers should *not* wade across here but instead walk northwest (slightly right) on a faint trail to a good log bridge. The time spent searching for this humble example of human engineering is worth keeping your feet dry. Resume the dirt trail west, then encounter a second, even more modest bridge. Pass a small meadow to your right with a few tent sites; the larger flat ground to your left is often well-fertilized by outfitters' horses. Soon after the meadow, look for the improbable sign to the falls: a simple, sawed-off log with the word "falls" carved into it. Turn left here, carefully ascending a stony trail for 0.1 mile to reach the falls where they burst through a narrow, rocky cleft. After taking photographs and perhaps enjoying lunch, return the same way.

To reach the lake, resume the main trail west for another 3.0 miles. The path gets steeper, especially as it crosses a minor ridge, but views of the tumbling mountain creek to the left make the effort worthwhile. About 4.0 miles from the car, encounter debris from a windstorm that uprooted mature pines; trail crews mostly cleared the path, but you may need to step over some logs. Wildflowers flourish in the newly formed meadows, especially in early- to mid-summer. The trail leads upward through a rocky area before the landscape opens to reveal the lake, flowering meadows, willows alive with songbirds, and mountains to either side. The best campsites are west of the lake, 100 feet or more from the water. You did remember your fly rod, right?

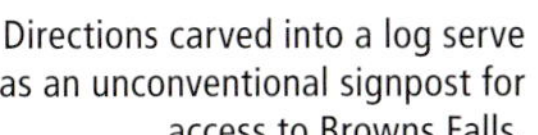

Directions carved into a log serve as an unconventional signpost for access to Browns Falls.

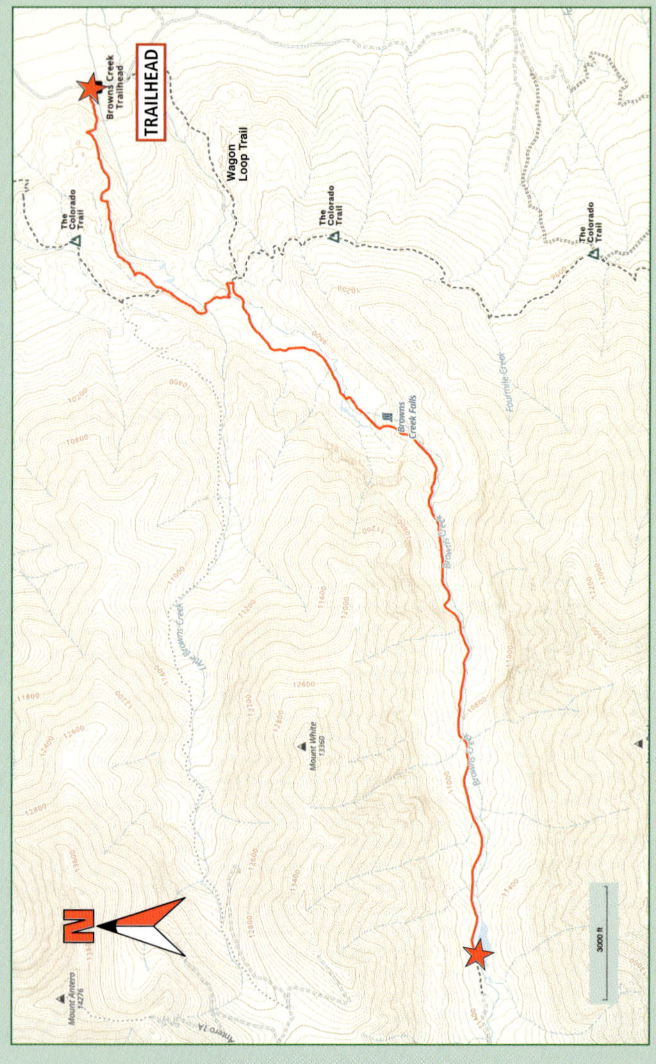
TRAILHEAD
Browns Creek Trailhead
Wagon Loop Trail
The Colorado Trail
The Colorado Trail
The Colorado Trail
Browns Creek Falls
Fourmile Creek
Browns Creek
Little Browns Creek
Browns Creek
Mount White 13360
Mount Antero 14276
3000 ft

17. Wagon Loop Trail

RATING	Moderate
ROUND-TRIP DISTANCE	3.25 miles
ROUND-TRIP TIME	2 to 3 hours
STARTING ELEVATION	8,900 feet
HIGHEST ELEVATION	9,670 feet
ELEVATION GAIN	770 feet
MAPS	Trails Illustrated #130 Salida/ St. Elmo
TRAILHEAD	Browns Creek Trailhead

COMMENT: Do this trail as a modest day hike through montane forests or as a slightly longer finish to the Browns Lake trek (this route follows parts of Browns Lake and the CT before bending onto its own path). Mountain bikers often share the Wagon Loop. The undulating terrain travels through diverse microecosystems, with the variety of trees and creekside plants in turn supporting mammals (deer, coyotes, and occasionally bear) and birds (depending on the season, Western tanagers, mountain chickadees, juncos, northern flickers, downy woodpeckers, ever-gossiping pine siskins, and nuthatches with their endless *yak-yak*). In autumn, the sun kisses the gold and red aspens and willows that flank them. Parts of this trail require ascending or descending loose rocks and gravel, which is why the short, mid-altitude hike is ranked moderate. Mountain bikers may rank it as difficult because on two wheels the route demands technical riding skills.

Dogs are allowed, with leashes recommended. Bird viewing is excellent. Wildflower viewing is moderate. The fall foliage is excellent. Fishing is marginal. Mountain bikers frequent this trail.

Wagon Loop Trail, popular with mountain bikers as well as hikers, connects to both the CT and Browns Creek Trail.

GETTING THERE: From US 285, turn west onto Chaffee County Road 270, which soon turns to dirt but remains passable to passenger cars. This turn is 15.4 miles north of the US 285/US 50 intersection near Poncha Springs, 2.5 miles south of the junction of US 285 and US 24, and 11.3 miles south of Buena Vista. Once on CR 270, drive west 1.5 miles to a four-way intersection. Go straight west on Forest Service Road 272 (do not turn right to stay on CR 270). Follow Forest Service Road 272 for 2.0 miles, then turn left. Drive about 1.5 miles to a large trailhead and a pit toilet. There is no potable water here.

THE HIKE: You can hike this loop from either direction, but it's described here so hikers returning from Browns Lake can follow it back as an alternative ending for their excursions. Walk west past the outhouse and follow the trail as if you're going to Browns Lake. About 1.4 miles from the trailhead, the Browns Lake Trail intersects the CT. Veer south (a left turn if you're hiking up from the parking lot). In 0.2 mile, cross Little Browns Creek on a good bridge. For the Wagon Loop, turn south onto the CT; coming from the car, that's a left; returning from Browns Lake it's a right. Follow the CT on a good dirt path for 0.15 mile to where it crosses the main Browns Creek, and for another 0.15 mile to the Wagon Loop junction. Again, turn left (east) and drop onto a rocky section. The trail has several of these loose, stony segments, so watch your footing (trekking poles really help). For the next 1.2 miles, the path rolls up and down small hills, crossing small streams on decent wood bridges and offering nature lovers opportunities to look for wildlife and birds. Encounter one annoying, stony uphill push, after which the path starts bending left (north) and becomes easier. Approximately 3.0 miles into the hike, the trail T-bones into the access road. Turn left (north) and walk 0.25 miles on the dirt road back to your car.

Wagon Loop Trail, seen here in early October, makes for a pleasant forest hike from late spring into early autumn.

N
The Colorado Trail
TRAILHEAD
Browns Creek Trailhead
Wagon Loop Trail
9400
9000
Browns Creek
Wagon Loop Trail 1427
Browns Creek
Browns Creek Trail
9400
9000
9400
The Colorado Trail
10200
9800
1000 ft

SALIDA AREA

Stunning views await hikers along the strenuous Continental Divide Trail west of Salida.

18. Mount Shavano and Tabeguache Peak

RATING	Difficult; strenuous; Class 2
ROUND-TRIP DISTANCE	9.0 miles for only Shavano; 10.0 miles with Tabeguache
ROUND-TRIP TIME	7 to 9 hours for Shavano only; 9 to 11 hours with Tabeguache
STARTING ELEVATION	9,750 feet
ENDING ELEVATION	14,229 feet (Shavano)
ELEVATION GAIN	4,500 feet for Shavano only; 5,600 feet if also hiking Tabeguache
MAPS	Trails Illustrated #130 Salida/ St. Elmo
TRAILHEAD	Shavano/Tabeguache Trailhead (Weldon Gulch Road access)

COMMENT: Shavano beckons from both US 285 and 50, but shy Tabeguache can't be seen clearly from the highways. This long, strenuous trek rewards tenacious hikers with great views of the Sawatch Range to the north and of Mount Ouray to the south. Just below timberline, hikers walk through groves of ancient bristlecone pines. The trail, steep for most of its length, means the descent taxes the leg muscles almost as much as the ascent; trekking poles are especially useful when going over loose gravel or talus. This route is the only approved way up either mountain; the Forest Service closed other trails that previously led directly to Tabeguache because of severe erosion and watershed damage.

GETTING THERE: From US 285, turn west onto Chaffee County Road 140. This junction is 1.0 mile north of the US 285/US 50 intersection near Poncha Springs and 21.0 miles south

The steep trail up Mount Shavano winds through an ancient bristlecone grove, then turns slightly north to ascend the ridge (on the right side of the photo). The winter route crosses the alpine bowl normally filled by the Angel of Shavano snow formation, then turns north (right) to the ridge. From there, the routes reach another north-trending ridge to the summit, which remains out of sight from this viewpoint.

of Buena Vista on US 285/US 24. The turn is marked by a brown sign stating "To Shavano and Tabeguache." Follow CR 140 for 1.7 miles to the junction with Chaffee County Road 250 and turn right. Drive 4.0 miles on CR 250; the road becomes dirt but remains passable to passenger cars. At a Y junction, head left on Forest Road 252. Drive another 3.2 miles, cross a cattleguard, and arrive at the trailhead, which has a pit toilet but no drinking water. Camping is prohibited at the trailhead, but you'll find many dispersed camping spots along the access roads; bring plenty of water for you and your pets.

Dogs on leash are allowed. Bird viewing is good. Wildflower viewing is fair, mostly along the first mile. Fall foliage is good. There is no fishing. Watch out for bears. Note

Take time on the descent to marvel at the centuries-old bristlecone pines, amazing survivors in a harsh, cold, arid, and windblown climate.

that the trail travels long distances above timberline and is exposed to thunderstorms and wind.

Read this book's Introduction for the meaning of Shavano and Tabeguache and for how to pronounce the latter's name.

THE HIKE: Start by sauntering through aspen groves along a spring-fed meadow and past the historic Blanks Cabin. After 0.1 mile, turn right onto the CT. After 0.25 mile,

Mount Shavano appears clearly from US 285, but Tabeguache Peak hides behind it.

reach another junction and turn left onto the well-signed Mount Shavano Trail. The path steepens as it winds through coniferous forest for 3.0 miles. Note the rounded rocks on and near the trail; they're evidence of erosion's endless work, which has transported millions of tons of debris down the mountain a few stones and sand grains at a time. Near timberline you'll pass bristlecone pines clinging to the rocky, sandy hillsides; read below to learn more about these durable, fascinating life-forms.

Emerge from the sheltering forest just under a shallow bowl, which normally harbors the Angel of Shavano snow formation from mid-winter through early summer. Above timberline, the rocky path contours for 0.9 mile along Shavano's south-facing shoulder, a place infamous for simultaneous cold wind and intense sun. The maintained trail ends at the 13,400-foot saddle below Shavano's summit, but generally the user-created route is easy to find as it veers right (north) along a weather-exposed ridge for 0.25 mile to the summit.

Check carefully for approaching bad weather before committing to Tabeguache. It's a 1.0-mile round-trip hike and another 1,000 feet of elevation loss and gain. If the weather

Wild roses grow along the lower stretches of Mount Shavano Trail.

cooperates, trudge down Shavano's rocky northwest shoulder to a saddle, then slog up Tabeguache's northeast shoulder. Go back the way you came.

Do *not* descend into McCoy Gulch! The south-facing gully below the Shavano/Tabegauche saddle is a trap that leads into a narrowing funnel of fallen timber and loose rock and ends in impassable cliffs. If you venture there, you'll likely have to call for rescue, then you'll make the local news, get trolled on social media, and probably have a nasty fight with your significant other. Just go back up and over Shavano; it's your only safe, reputation-saving option.

Bristlecone pines

These ancient, twisted, and slow-growing conifers thrive at high altitudes and in sandy soils where most plants can't even take root. In fact, the bristlecone's slow rate of growth likely lets them endure droughts as well as extreme winters. Some of these trees on Mount Shavano may be 2,000 years old. The short needles of the bristlecone pine sprout in groups of five, giving their branches a brushy appearance. Their dark-purple female cones sport slender tips (hence the name bristlecone). Although not exactly rare, their numbers are much fewer than more abundant pines like ponderosa or lodgepole. Enjoy looking and taking pictures of these unusual trees, but don't break off branches or cones, either of which may represent decades of growth during harsh conditions.

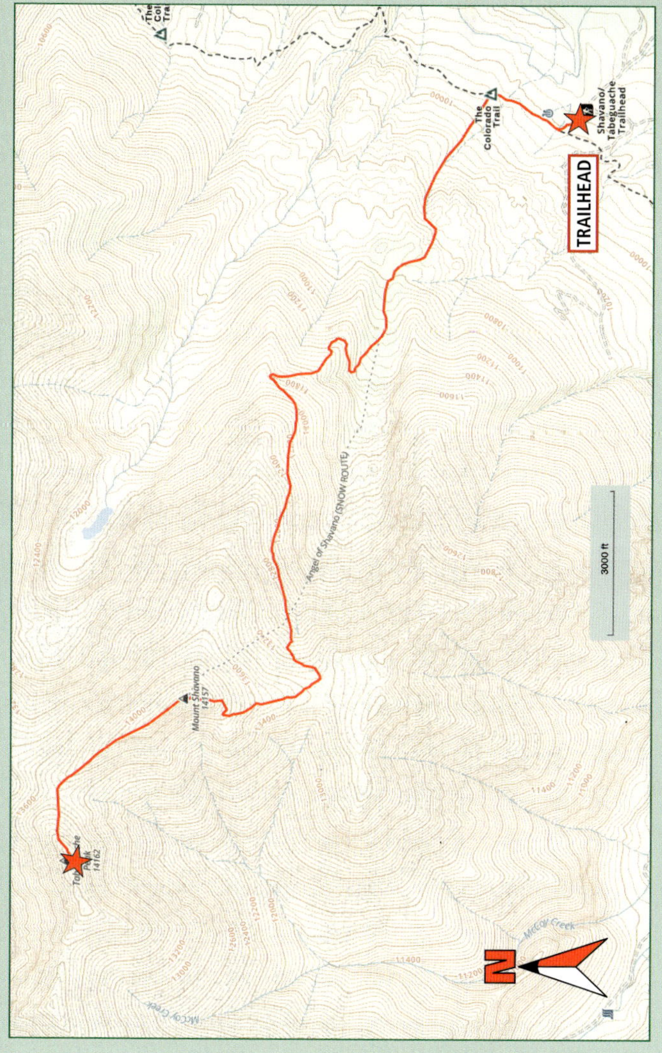
TRAILHEAD
Shavano/
Tabeguache
Trailhead
The
Colorado
Trail
Angel of Shavano (SNOW ROUTE)
Mount Shavano
14157
14162
3000 ft
McCoy Creek
N

19. Greens Creek Trail

RATING	Moderate
ROUND-TRIP DISTANCE	13.5 miles; much shorter option available
ROUND-TRIP TIME	7 to 9 hours (full hike); 2 to 4 hours (partial hike)
STARTING ELEVATION	8,570 feet
ENDING ELEVATION	11,500 feet
ELEVATION GAIN	2,900 feet
MAPS	Trails Illustrated #130 Salida/ St. Elmo and #139 La Garita/ Cochetopa Hills
TRAILHEAD	County Road 221 access

COMMENT: This trail's proximity to Salida and its relatively low-elevation trailhead make it popular year-round for hikers, mountain bikers, and horseback riders. Wildflowers and birds enjoy the riparian ecosystem from early spring to late summer, while aspens and wetlands turn fabulous colors in autumn. The first few miles offer an easy walk, so many hikers travel only partway to the crest. More ambitious trekkers push to where the Greens Creek Trail intersects the CT atop the Continental Divide. From that highpoint, hikers can backtrack (no car shuttle required), or link to the CT, CDT, Monarch Crest Loop, and the Fooses Creek Trails, but the longer journeys require shuttles and overnight backpacking.

Dogs on leash are allowed. Bird viewing is excellent. Wildflower and fall foliage viewing are also excellent. Fishing is marginal. Look sharp for moose and mountain bikers. Watch out for poison ivy (irritating) and Western hemlock (all parts of the plant are toxic) next to the creek in the first few miles.

The lower part of Greens Creek Trail, seen here, can be accessed most of the year, but in winter snow blankets the upper hillsides where the path connects to the CDT and CT.

GETTING THERE: From the intersection of US 50 and 285 near Poncha Springs, drive west on US 50 for 2.1 miles. Turn left (south) on Chaffee County 220; a sign for a local winery also marks this turn (as of 2020). Drive 1.7 miles southwest on CR 220 to a junction with Chaffee County Road 221; stay left on CR 220, heeding the helpful sign that points to the Greens Creek Trail. Drive just under 1.0 mile on CR 220 (dodging mountain bikers on the way) and park in a small dirt lot on the road's right side. The trail starts near the creek. Passenger cars can handle the dirt road to the trailhead, but past here CR 220 devolves into a four-wheel-drive track that's rough even for SUVs.

THE HIKE: The generally smooth trail starts by following close to the creek for about 2.0 miles, occasionally wandering up open hillsides with views looking north to the mountains and down into the creek. Wildflowers bloom along these early miles from mid-spring into late summer, while the plentiful aspens and willows sport intense fall colors. A variety of song birds cluster near the creek and along the drier hillsides.

Greens Creek creates riparian habitat for an array of flowers, birds, fascinating insects, and animals ranging in size from mice to moose.

Greens Creek makes a nice wildflower hike in late spring and early summer, and a colorful leaf-peeping trek in autumn.

A side stream enters Greens Creek about 2.3 miles into the hike, after which the trail begins to climb earnestly and the path becomes much rockier. Many day hikers turn around at this point for a nice 4.6-mile, out-and-back excursion. Hardier hikers continue up the steeping path, crossing Greens Creek and ascending to the junction with the CT and CDT. Enjoy the great views.

TRAILHEAD
0
1
MILES
N
sabel National Forest

20. Boss Lake (classic approach)

RATING	Moderate
ROUND-TRIP DISTANCE	4.8 miles (from the two-wheel-drive parking); 1.8 miles (from the upper four-wheel-drive parking)
ROUND-TRIP TIME	3 to 4 hours (from the two-wheel-drive parking); 1 to 3 hours (from the upper parking)
STARTING ELEVATION	9,590 feet (two-wheel-drive parking); 9,890 (four-wheel-drive parking)
ENDING ELEVATION	10,866 feet (Boss Lake)
ELEVATION GAIN	1,270 feet (from the two-wheel-drive parking); 975 feet (from the end of four-wheel-drive road)
MAPS	Trails Illustrated #130 Salida/ St. Elmo
TRAILHEAD	Middle Fork Road access

COMMENT: The Boss Lake trail offers striking views from atop a waterfall and down the US 50 corridor into the river valley; the stream that flows from this lake is a key tributary to the South Arkansas River. Hikers usually combine a trip to Boss Lake—which is a natural lake that expanded after construction of man-made dam—with a trek to nearby all-natural Hunt Lake. These destinations are just 2.3 miles apart. Good picnic spots flank Boss Lake's south and eastern shores, but legal tent sites (more than 100 feet from the water) are scarce; you'll find better camping around Hunt Lake. But the best thing about Boss Lake is standing on the bridge over the Middle Fork of the Arkansas River with the waterfall gushing right below your feet.

Dogs are allowed, with leashes recommended. Bird viewing and wildflower viewing are good. Fall foliage is excellent.

Boss Lake Trail looks down the South Arkansas River drainage.

Be wary of loose rock on the road from the two-wheel-drive parking area; beetle-killed pines, which can fall in high winds; and winter avalanche hazard above the lake. A special note on fishing: Both Boss and Hunt Lakes are strictly catch and release. CPW is trying to recover the endangered, native greenback cutthroat trout, and these two lakes are key to that ongoing effort. Also, use only artificial flies and lures.

GETTING THERE: From the intersection of US 285 and US 50 in Poncha Springs, drive west on US 50 for 13.0 miles to the tiny town of Garfield. Turn right (north) on signed Forest Road 230 (also known as the Middle Fork Road). The best landmark for the turn is the snowmobile rental business on the highway's south side. (Note: this is *not* the road to Taylor Mountain.) After leaving the highway, drive northwest for less than 100 yards to a small parking area on your left, among the trees. All two-wheel-drive cars must, and SUVs should, park here unless their owners want to populate the rough road ahead with assorted souvenirs like an oil pan or

Fishing is strictly catch-and-release at Boss Lake to protect a native endangered trout species.

U-joint. ATVs and "lifted" SUVs with short wheelbases can handle the road, but drivers still must take care.

THE HIKE: Walk the four-wheel-drive road that leads uphill from the parking lot. About 0.5 mile into the hike, pass a side road on the right (east); don't turn. Continue on the main road, traveling slightly northwest. Cross two small side streams coming downhill from the right (north). To the left (south) a much larger stream cuts a deep cleft through the rock. This is the Middle Fork of the South Fork of the Arkansas River (locals call it the Middle Fork). About 1.5 miles from the parking area, reach a sign for the Boss Lake Trail. Go left (south) at the sign; if you miss this turn, you'll trudge miles along the road toward Hancock Lakes. Cross the four-wheel-drive/ATV parking lot. The trail continues to the left, behind a Forest Service information sign. Huff and puff up the last steep hill. Cross the Middle Fork's waterfall on a good bridge and reach the dam. Enjoy the view. From Boss Lake, you can keep hiking another 2.3 miles to Hunt Lake. Turn left from the Boss Lake Dam, then carefully cross the stream. Walk clockwise (south then west) around Boss Lake, then follow an old road for less than a mile to a junction with an ATV route. Turn right (west). Hike west on an old road for another 1 mile to Hunt Lake and better camping sites.

A mighty river flows from small tributaries like this stream, which feeds into the South Arkansas River—known to locals as "the Middle Fork."

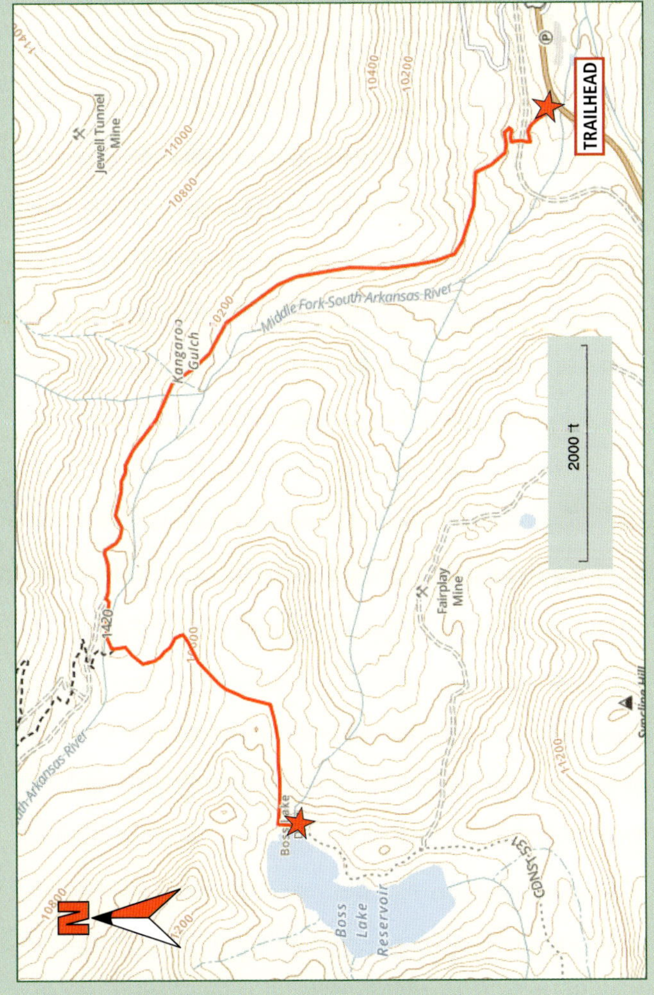
TRAILHEAD
Jewell Tunnel Mine
Middle Fork-South Arkansas River
Kangaroo Gulch
Fairplay Mine
Boss Lake Reservoir
2000 ft
N

21. Waterdog Lakes

RATING	Moderate
ROUND-TRIP DISTANCE	3.2 miles (to the first lake); 3.5 miles (including the upper lake)
ROUND-TRIP TIME	1.5 to 2 hours (to the first lake); 2 to 3 hours (to the upper lake)
STARTING ELEVATION	10,350 feet
ENDING ELEVATION	11,050 feet (first lake); 11,500 feet (upper lake)
ELEVATION GAIN	700 feet (to the first lake); 1,150 feet (to the upper lake)
MAPS	Trails Illustrated #130 Salida/ St. Elmo
TRAILHEAD	US 50 access

COMMENT: This trail, popular with snowshoers in winter, leads to two scenic lakes and impressive views of the Continental Divide. The path parallels and crosses mountain streams; wildflowers flank both from spring into fall, but peak in June and July. The first lake resides at the end of a clearly marked trail and remains relatively safe into winter. The upper lake can be reached only by following user-created trails, and the cliffs above it could present winter avalanche risk. The trek never gets really steep to either lake, but even the developed trail to the first lake climbs relentlessly and gets rocky in place. So, despite its short length, this charming trail merits a moderate rating. Find good spots for picnics and camping along the south and west lake shores. If no anglers are around, your pup also may enjoy a refreshing swim.

Dogs are allowed. Bird viewing is good. Wildflower viewing is excellent. Fishing is good, especially in the upper lake. Note that the riskiest part of the hike is crossing US 50 from the parking area on the south side to the obscure trailhead on the northside. Consider wearing bright colors.

Despite popular opinion, Waterdog Lakes were not named after dogs who love to swim. A waterdog is a kind of native salamander.

GETTING THERE: From the intersection of US 50 and US 285 near Poncha Springs, drive west on US 50 about 16.25 miles and look for a small, unmarked gravel parking area on the left (south) side of the road. This spot is past Monarch Lodge, but if you reach the ski area, you've gone too far. After you park, cross the highway carefully; aim left of the "keep right" sign and right of the "curves ahead" sign. The trailhead hides behind the trees.

THE HIKE: The first few steep steps after the trail sign hint at the nearly continuous climb ahead. After a few hundred yards, ignore the dead-end side trail to the creek. Keep walking uphill through a clearing under power poles intermittently posted with blue diamond winter trail markers. After about 1.0 mile, decide which small logs are most stable to cross a small stream. Contour along a hill. At about 1.4 miles, hop on rocks to cross the next creek. Marsh marigolds and other water-loving flowers hug the creek sides; you also may spot some blue columbines. The trail curves slightly as it ascends the last 0.2 mile to the first lake. Dogs love to play at the sandy beach, while hikers will find good places to picnic in the trees along the south shore. No real trail leads to the second lake. However, a

Decent campsites dot the shores of the lower of the two Waterdog Lakes.

small user-created trail leads counterclockwise (east) through the trees, around the first lake and up the second bench, where better fishing can be found in the upper lake.

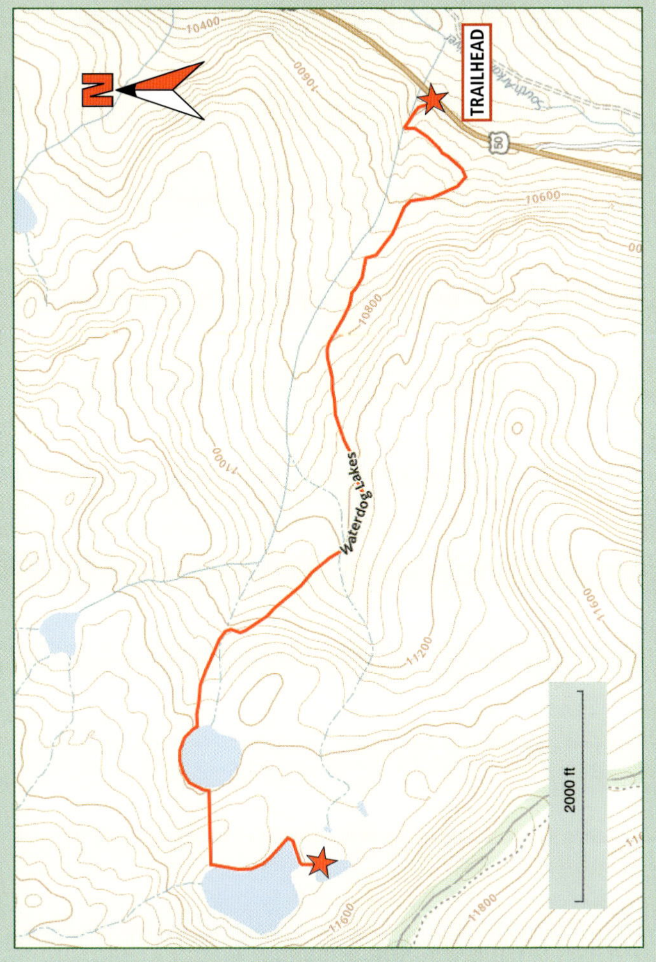
TRAILHEAD
Waterdog Lakes
2000 ft
10400
10600
10800
11000
11200
11600
11800
50

22. Continental Divide Trail/ Colorado Trail Collegiate West Segment 5

RATING	Difficult
ROUND-TRIP DISTANCE	22.4 miles; 11.2 miles one-way with shuttle (recommended)
ROUND-TRIP TIME	13 hours to 15 hours (round-trip); 6 to 12 hours (one-way)
STARTING ELEVATION	11,386 feet
HIGHEST ELEVATION	12,515 feet
ELEVATION GAIN/LOSS	1,429 feet (gain); 2,640 feet (loss)
MAPS	Trails Illustrated #130 Salida/ St. Elmo/Mount Shavano
TRAILHEAD	Old Monarch Pass Road access

COMMENT: In a land of exquisite beauty, this trail offers especially glorious scenery: 360-degree vistas of four mountain ranges, sweeping tundra, scenic mountain tarns, old-growth forest, and a mountain lake surrounded by grassy wetlands. Hikers must labor for this lofty reward, however, because the challenging trek stays mostly above timberline and is seriously exposed to lightning, fierce winds, and summer snows. Low clouds (fog) and lingering or early snowfields can obscure the trail, making good navigation skills essential. A car shuttle is the best way to tackle this trail. Start the hike at Old Monarch Pass and drop to Chaffee County Road 235. With an early start, you should be heading down when afternoon thunderstorms strike. This trek is part of the CDT and the CT's Collegiate West Segment 5, so you will experience a fraction of the long journey atop North America's backbone.

Dogs are allowed on leash. Bird viewing is good. Wildflower viewing is excellent in early summer. The fall foliage is good.

Views from the CDT are breathtaking both because hikers can see for about 100 miles and because this section's elevation stays over 12,000 feet most of the trek.

Fishing is subject to special restrictions in Hunt and Boss Lakes. Keep an eye out for weather and avalanches from late fall to late spring.

GETTING THERE: For the lower shuttle/hike's end: From the junction of US 285 and US 50 near Poncha Springs, drive west 21.0 miles to the obscure turnoff for Chaffee County Road 235. This turn is less than 1.0 mile west of Garfield; it exits the paved road just before the highway department's storage barn on the right (if you see the barn, you just passed CR 235). When you find it, turn northeast onto CR 235. Drive 100 yards to an unmarked dirt road junction on your left; passenger cars and all-wheel-drive vehicles should park here (don't block the road). SUVs can turn left on the dirt road (CR 235's continuation) and follow the rougher track to an informal campsite among the aspens, and SUVs that are not lifted should claim one of the two or three parking spots here. This place is at the bottom of a hill, just before the road curves northwest. From here, CR 235 mutates into a ridiculous excuse for a road suitable only for ATVs and lunar rovers.

For the upper shuttle/hike's start: Drive west on US 50 to the well-signed turnoff for Old Monarch Pass; this junction

From the Divide, the CDT drops steeply down rocky switchbacks to alpine tarns.

is 5.0 miles west of CR 235 (or 26.0 miles from the stoplight at US 285 and US 50). Go 1.5 miles on the dirt Old Monarch Pass Road (passable to passenger cars from summer to early fall). Stop at the pass near a Forest Service sign. On your right (northeast) is a metal gate with CDT/CT markers.

THE HIKE: Walk around the gate and follow the unnamed dirt road uphill. Complete two switchbacks. Look on your right for an unmarked summer maintenance road. Follow this dirt and grass road uphill into Monarch Ski area, which will be obvious. Bend slightly left (west) up to the Continental Divide on a dirt trail. A tad west of the Divide, turn right (north) and follow the obvious path. The CDT/CT undulates near the exposed alpine ridge for 5.0 miles, usually staying a bit west of the Divide but sometimes striding directly atop the continent's backbone. Pass under a powerline. Cross above several ski runs. Pass a lift sitting right atop the Divide.

About 0.5 mile north of this high ski lift, the CDT/CT exits the road left at a junction; look for a small trail marker. In 0.3 mile from the turn, walk left and uphill on another dirt road. In another 0.8 mile, trudge right (slightly northeast) and

Hunt Lake offers the best campsites along this part of the CDT.

uphill to a horizontal metal sign, which explains the Native peoples' prehistoric hunts. From the sign, the trail again turns left (north). Pass another small powerline. Look down onto Waterdog Lakes. Pass a cairn, and reach your highpoint on Bald Mountain's bulky flank. Continue north. Look for a giant rock cairn at a notch in the ridge: Do not miss this turn. From the cairn (elevation 12,470 feet), turn right (east). Descend 0.7 mile on steep, rocky, and sometimes muddy or icy switchbacks.

Reach glistening alpine tarns (elevation 11,900 feet); there is no comfortable camping here. Ramble down 0.6 mile into the ancient forest surrounding Hunt Lake where you'll find nice campsites. From Hunt Lake, stroll 1.1 miles to a T-intersection. Veer right (east) on CR 235. Grunt over boulders, potholes, and mud puddles for 2.0 miles to the four-wheel-drive parking, or walk the road a bit farther to your vehicle. From Hunt Lake, stroll 1.1 miles to a T-intersection. Veer right (east) on CR 235. Continue for 2.0 miles to the four-wheel drive parking, or continue walking the road a bit farther to your two-wheel-drive vehicle. (Turning left [north] at the T-intersection leads to Boss Lake and the rest of the CDT, from where you could trek north all the way to Canada, eh?)

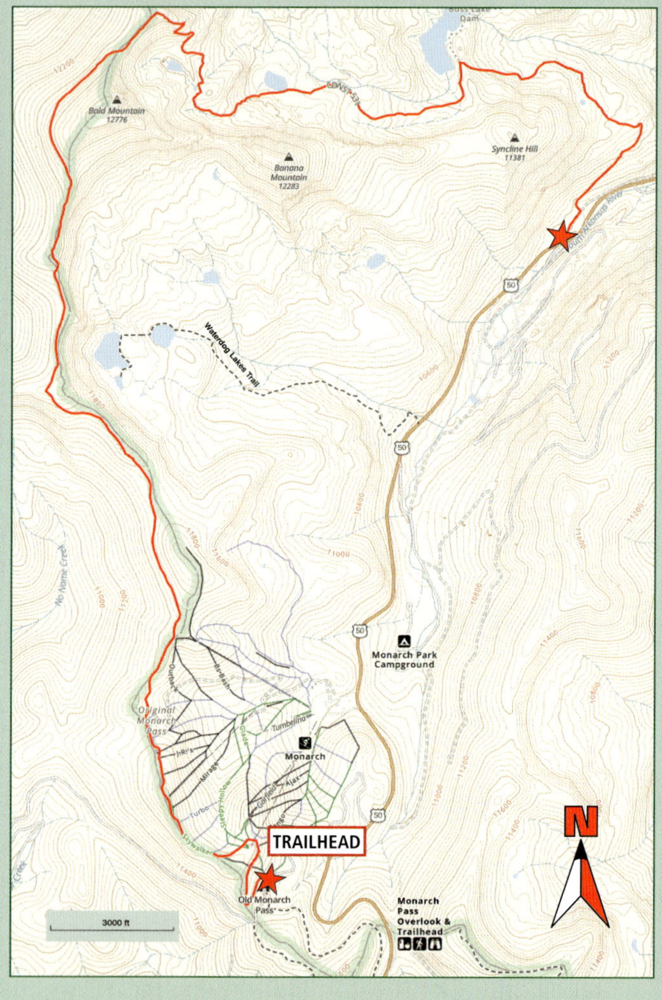

Bald Mountain
12776
Banana Mountain
12283
Syncline Hill
11381
Waterdog Lakes Trail
Monarch Park Campground
Original Monarch Pass
Monarch
TRAILHEAD
Old Monarch Pass
Monarch Pass Overlook & Trailhead
No Name Creek
3000 ft
N

23. Mount Ouray

RATING	Difficult; time-consuming Class 2 on the ridge
ROUND-TRIP DISTANCE	6.4 miles
ROUND-TRIP TIME	7 hours to 9.5 hours
STARTING ELEVATION	10,820 feet
ENDING ELEVATION	13,971 feet
ELEVATION GAIN	3,240
MAPS	Trails Illustrated #139 La Garita/ Cochetopa Hills
TRAILHEAD	Marshall Pass Road access

COMMENT: Mount Ouray is a good introduction to Colorado's high 13ers, especially because the 13ers, on the whole, are harder than most 14ers. The west ridge route described here is easier to follow than other options to the east, but no official trail leads to the summit from any direction. While most of the route is just walking, the last 1,400 feet of loose rock is time-consuming, so build a few extra hours into your schedule.

Dogs are allowed but should be able to handle rocky terrain. Bird viewing is good. Wildflower viewing is fair. Fall foliage is good. Fishing is available only in ponds below the access road. This route has unpredictable weather and navigation challenges.

GETTING THERE: From the north, drive south on US 285. From the junction with US 50, continue south on US 285 for 5.3 miles. Turn southwest (right) on Marshall Pass/Forest Service Road 200 to O'Haver Lake. From the south, drive US 285 north over Poncha Pass, continue for 2.3 miles, then turn southwest (left) onto Marshall Pass/Forest Service Road 200. From the Forest Service Road 200 turnoff, pass the lake and camp-

The easiest way up Mount Ouray ascends the left side ridge, but no official trail leads to the summit.

ground and drive 13.4 miles toward Marshall Pass. Don't go all the way to the pass unless it's the only place to park. If possible, stash your car 0.1 mile east of the pass near a pit toilet with a small lot. Exit your vehicle, turn around, and look at the tree and grass slope to the north: that's your mountain.

THE HIKE: Your first goal is to reach Mount Ouray's long west ridge. Find the small dirt four-wheel-drive track (Forest Road 200C) that leads uphill across from the pit toilet; the walk starts gently uphill from here. (This track is *not* the four-wheel-drive road farther west, which is part of the CT/CDT. Your route instead starts east of the pass and does not have any CT/CDT markers.) Less than 1.0 mile from your car, walk by the historic Hutchinson and Burnett cabin at an elevation of roughly 10,900 feet. Bear right, still following the old road. Where the trail fades into a faint track, walk as efficiently as you can through widely spaced spruce trees for 0.8 mile toward the west ridge, reaching timberline at about 11,800 feet. Continue for another 0.2 mile toward the Continental Divide. Once on the Divide, bear right (northeast) on Ouray's high ridgeline. Stay close to the ridge's top, trek over alternating grass and rocks, and plod over a terrain hump. At about 12,500 feet, encounter a loose, rocky spine; this obstacle is the hike's crux and starts a nearly 1,400-foot Class 2 section. Bypass the stony rib to its left on the ascent (right on the descent). When you can, get back on the ridge. Totter toward the top along moderate but wobbly talus. Enjoy the expansive view before returning the way you came.

Note: Walking down 1,400 feet of rocky terrain with uncertain footing consumes more time than you might expect. The talus is too unstable to run on and too shallow to plunge step. Get an early start on this beautiful, isolated peak, and don't rush the descent.

Mount Ouray's eastern side, known as the Armchair, is a classic glacier-carved geologic feature.

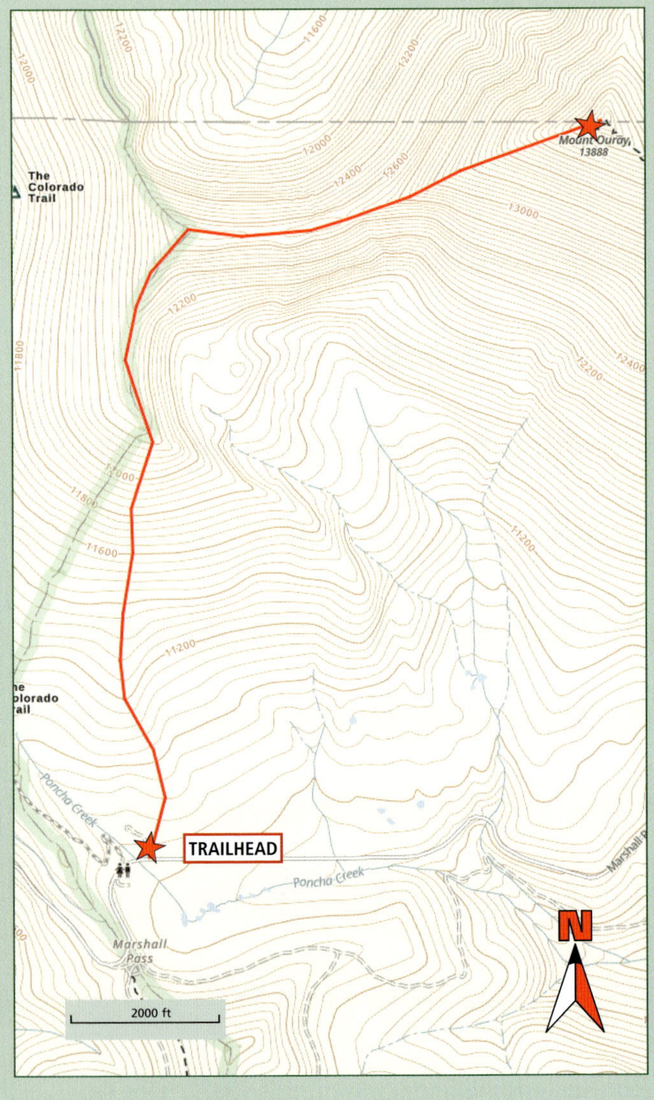

Mount Ouray
13888
The Colorado Trail
The Colorado Trail
Poncha Creek
Poncha Creek
TRAILHEAD
Marshall Pass
2000 ft
N

24. Little Rainbow Trail

RATING	Full distance (CR110 to Burmac Road) round-trip: difficult; one-way: moderate. CR110 to CR108 round-trip: moderate; one-way: easy. CR108 to Burmac Road round-trip: moderate; one-way: easy.
ROUND-TRIP DISTANCE	*Car shuttle recommended.* Round-trip: 12.6 miles (9.6 miles on Little Rainbow with 3 miles on the Race Track trail). One way: 6.3 miles (4.8 miles on Little Rainbow, with 1.5 miles on Race Track trail).
First shorter option:	CR110 to CR108: 6.2 miles round-trip; 3.1 miles one-way, all on Little Rainbow.
Second shorter option, CR108 to Burmac Road:	7 miles round-trip (4 miles on Little Rainbow, 3 miles on Race Track); 3.5 one-way with shuttle (2 miles on Little Rainbow, 1.5 miles on Race Track).
ROUND-TRIP TIME	7.5–11 hours (round-trip, full distance); 4–5 hours (one-way, full distance). CR110 to CR108 option: 3–4 hours (round-trip); 1.5–2.5 hours (one-way). CR108 to Burmac Road trailhead: 2.5–4 hours round-trip; 1.5–2 hours one-way.
STARTING ELEVATION	7,880 feet (west trailhead)
ENDING ELEVATION	7,560 feet (east trailhead)
ELEVATION GAIN	410 feet up; 900 feet down (west to east)
MAPS	Trails Illustrated #130 Salida/St. Elmo; Trails Illustrated #138 Sangre de Cristo/Great Sand Dunes
TRAILHEAD	Little Rainbow Trailhead (West Trailhead)

Little Rainbow Trail travels through arid pinyon and juniper forests while offering open views of the Upper Arkansas River Valley to the north.

COMMENT: Four important notes: 1) This trail is popular with mountain bikes, so keep your eyes open. 2) Several shorter trails intersect Little Rainbow, so you can create your own loops after you grow familiar with the area. 3) Trails south of Powerline Road close from December 1 to April 15 to protect wildlife habitat. 4) Bring plenty of water because there's none at the parking lots or on the trails.

Located on Methodist Mountain's north slopes, the Little Rainbow Trail offers an easier alternative to the main Rainbow Trail, so it's better suited for families and casual hikers. I recommend a one-way hike, using car shuttles—otherwise, the distances make for a genuine workout. Even for shorter distances, this trail provides great north-facing vistas including the Upper Arkansas River Valley and surrounding mountain ranges. The path ambles through pinyon forests, over small hills and across seasonal creeks. DOGS: Yes, if leashed. BIRDS: Good. WILDFLOWERS: Moderate. FALL FOLIAGE: Good. FISHING: None. BE AWARE: Mountain bikes. Bring lots of water. Don't approach rabbits or other wild animals that may carry diseases.

GETTING THERE: Some area maps are now outdated because new housing developments have sprung up near the trails, but you should find the trailheads (accessible to passenger cars in most seasons) with these directions. **For the western Little Rainbow Trailhead:** From U.S. 50/Rainbow Drive in Salida, turn south on Chaffee County Road 110 at a brown sign that says "Methodist Mountain Trails;" as of 2024, a WalMart is across (north) of the turn. Drive 2.3 miles on the winding CR110 over the South Arkansas River and past several junctions. CR110 becomes BLM route 5668; just keep going. About 1.5 miles from the highway, pass the large Spartan trail parking (with pit toilet) on your right. Stay on CR110/BLM 5668 for another 0.8 mile up a short hill where a road sign points to a trailhead; turn left here into the western Little Rainbow Trailhead parking area. There's no pit toilet here and no water.

The shorter options: From US 50/Rainbow Drive in Salida, turn south on Chaffee County Road 107 just before a stoplight. Pass the 107A junction and several private residential roads/driveways. CR107 soon becomes CR108. About 3.6 miles from the highway, the Little Rainbow Trail crosses CR108. Park the shuttle car here. (If you reach Powerline Road, you missed it).

Little Rainbow Trail is popular with locals because it's so close to Salida, seen here.

For the eastern Little Rainbow Trailhead: From the Salida Hot Springs and Aquatic Center in Salida, drive east on US 50 for 2.4 miles and turn south on Burmac Road; if you pass the Salida East Recreation Area, you missed it. A few dozen yards from the US 50/Burmac junction, veer right to avoid the lumber company's parking lot. Follow the public road about 0.25 mile to a BLM access sign; turn left into a large parking lot.

THE HIKE: From west to east, the trail trends downhill while undulating over small hills and drainages. It's joyful walking—never steep, just a bit of uphill to work the lungs, some downhill to provide a short rest, then the sequence repeats. The path meanders among pinyon pines, yucca, and sagebrush; song birds love these food sources, so look and listen carefully. When the forest opens a bit, enjoy great views of the Arkansas River Valley, the high mountains to the west, the Buffalo Peaks in the far northeast, and Salida below you. About 0.3 mile from the start, intersect the Skull Trail but stay on the Little Rainbow Trail heading generally east. Approximately 2 miles from your car, Little Rainbow intersects both the Spartan and Solstice trails; stay on Little Rainbow. In another 0.8 mile, your trail meets CR108. If you followed my recommendation, you parked a shuttle car here.

If not, continue east on the Little Rainbow for 1.1 miles to the Lost Trail, but please don't get lost. Instead, head east another 0.9 mile to a three-way junction with a dirt road and the Race Track and Dead Bird trails. Pick any of them for the descent to the parking lot; they're all about 2.8 miles. The road is boring but offers easy walking. Dead Bird leads out of your way as it bends back to the Lost Trail before heading to the parking lot. Race Track is the shortest but most sporting option as you may dodge speeding bikes.

If you didn't shuttle, then trudge back to the CR110 parking area—but you only need to make a full-length, round trip if you want a strenuous hike or, ahem, are writing a guidebook.

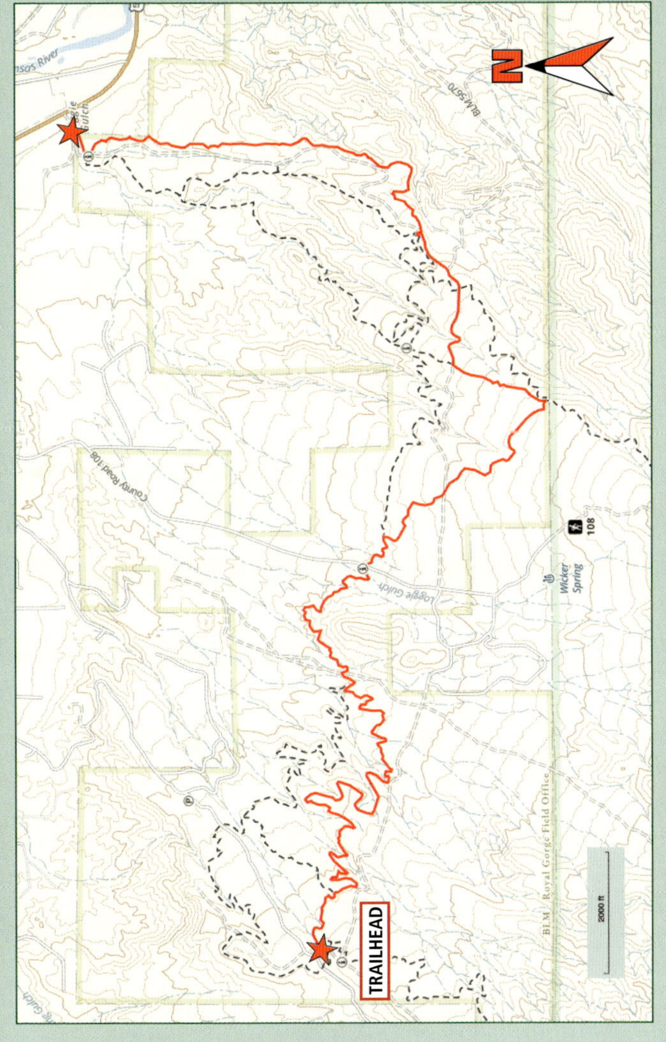
TRAILHEAD
County Road 108
Loggie Gulch
Wicker Spring
108
BLM 5670
BLM Royal Gorge Field Office
2000 ft

25. Rainbow Trail

RATING	Difficult (full length) to moderate (shorter sections)
ROUND-TRIP DISTANCE	31 miles (shorter options available, see note below)
ROUND-TRIP TIME	16–23 hours (shorter options available, see note below)
STARTING ELEVATION	8,860 feet
HIGHEST ELEVATION	10,250 feet (Poncha Mountain)
ENDING ELEVATION	8,560 feet
ELEVATION GAIN	2,775 feet gain; 2,300 feet loss (full-length of Salida area trail); route travels over many hills/drainages. Some 1,500 feet of the uphill involves the 3.5 miles from Mears Junction to Poncha Mountain. The rest of the trail wanders moderately up and down short hills and creek banks.
MAPS	Trails Illustrated #130 Salida/St. Elmo; Trails Illustrated #138 Sangre de Cristo/Great Sand Dunes
TRAILHEAD	Mears Junction on US 285

The famous Rainbow Trail (Forest Service Trail #1336) extends more than 100 miles and connects communities from Salida to Westcliffe, forming a long, rainbow-shaped arc on the east side of the Sangre de Cristo Range's east side. Almost all hikers, trail runners, and even mountain bikers break this trail into shorter, manageable day trips. This chapter covers just the first one-third of the trail closest to Salida. Most of the Rainbow Trail undulates moderately, but in the Salida area the steepest stretches are near Poncha Mountain, a few miles east of US 285. ***Pack plenty of water*** because there's none at the trailheads and some of the streams you cross flow only in spring and early summer.

The US Forest Service, other government agencies, and local volunteer groups such as Salida Mountain Trails removed most of the debris and dangerous dead trees following the 2019 Methodist Mountain wildfire, but you should stay alert because the wind still could topple some of the remaining burned pines. In addition, the agencies and volunteers revamped the affected trailheads, chainsawed through fallen logs, and added helpful new signage. Appreciate their work as you saunter along this long path with its ever-changing views, great bird and wildlife habitat, and newly opened meadows filled with seasonal wildflowers.

As noted in the Little Rainbow Trail chapter, new housing developments on Methodist Mountain's north-facing slopes have created a maze of private streets and driveways, so don't rely on old maps. Access to the old Forest Service Road 124 effectively has been blocked. So, these days, the best day hikes on the Rainbow Trail are the ones described below. This is why you buy a guidebook: because the author researched the "ground truth."

Two other notes: 1) Dirt bikes also legally use this part of the Rainbow Trail; although they're supposed to yield to pedestrians, some don't, so use common sense and stay safe. 2) The Forest Service closes access to the Rainbow Trail for all users from December 1 to April 15 to protect wildlife. Please respect this eco-sensitive closure.

A NOTE ON TRIP DISTANCES AND HIKING TIMES: All mileage and hiking times are calculated from Mears Junction on US 285 to the Bear Creek parking area on Fremont County Road 49. The total elevation gain/loss includes the bend around Poncha Peak, several small hills, and numerous stream drainages.

Part of the Rainbow Trail overlooks US 285 and O'Haver Lake near Poncha Springs.

Full distance, round-trip, Mears Junction to Bear Creek: 31 miles. Hiking time: 16 hours to 23 hours. Difficult (i.e. length and Poncha Peak).

Full distance, Mears Jct. to Bear Creek, one-way with shuttle: 15.5 miles. Hiking time: 8 hours to 12 hours. Difficult.

First shorter option/shuttle: Mears Junction to Forest Service Road 108. For passenger cars and small AWD vehicles: 20 miles round-trip, 10 miles one-way with shuttle; includes 1 mile of 4WD road walking from parking by CR108. Hiking time: 10 hours (round-trip) to 5 hours (with shuttle at Bear Creek). Difficult (round-trip) to moderate (with shuttle). For true SUVs (11 inches of clearance and low gears: 18 miles round-trip, 9 miles one-way with shuttle. 9 hours (round-trip) to 4.5 hours (shuttle). Difficult (round-trip) to moderate (one-way, with shuttle).

Second shorter option/shuttle: FR108 to Bear Creek Trailhead/Fremont CR49. For passenger cars, 15 miles round-trip, 7.5 miles one-way with shuttle (includes 1 mile on 4WD road from CR108 to Loggie Gulch and 0.5 mile to junction with east-bound Bear Creek section). Difficult (round-trip) to moderate (with shuttle). For SUVs/4WD: 13 miles round-trip, 6.5 miles one-way. Difficult (round-trip) to moderate (with shuttle).

COMMENT: A local favorite, the Rainbow Trail is close to town, has relatively easy access, and offers great views of Salida, the Sawatch Range's 14ers, the Chalk Cliffs, Buffalo Peaks, and the head of Bighorn Canyon. The 31-mile trail section described in this chapter is challenging because of its length and steep slog around Poncha Mountain. But most of it is moderate, especially if broken into several, shorter day hikes—which is what almost everyone does, with car

Spacious and easy to follow, the Rainbow Trail is popular year-round with locals.

The Rainbow Trail offers expansive vistas, including great views of the Sawatch Range to the north.

shuttles from US 285, Chaffee County Road 108, or Chaffee County 101/Fremont County 49. A backpacking trip is possible but water sources are scarce—and do NOT camp in the burned areas, where dead trees could topple onto your tent. DOGS: Yes, if leashed. BIRDS: Excellent. WILDFLOWERS: Great, especially in the burned forest. (Yes, really—watch Mother Nature heal herself!) FALL FOLIAGE: Good. FISHING: None. BE AWARE: Part of the hike leads through burned forest. Watch out for mountain bikes and motorized dirt bikes.

GETTING THERE: I'll first describe how to get to the western and eastern trailheads for a full-length hike, then explain how to find Loggie Gulch and Columbine trailheads for shorter alternatives.

For the western/Mears Junction Trailhead: Paved, accessible to passenger cars. From the junction of US 50/US 285 in Poncha Springs, head south on US 285 for 5 miles. Pass the turnoff to O'Haver Lake/Road 200. Look for the Mears Junction historical marker on your right/west. You may blow by this obscure spot the first time; just use caution when turning around at the next pullout. Carefully pull off the road at the historical marker on the west side of US 295, or into the small parking area on the highway's east shoulder. After parking, look east/south for a brown-and-yellow trailhead sign amid the bushes.

For the eastern/ Bear Creek trailhead: Paved or good gravel/dirt roads accessible to passenger cars most of the way. From the Hot Springs and Aquatic Center in Salida, drive east on US 50 for just over 4 miles and turn south on Chaffee County Road 101. This exit is east of the Salida East Recreation Area and across the highway from the Arkansas River's Bear Creek Rapid. Follow CR101/Bear Creek to a small Y junction; go right on the main road as it curves. At a second Y, again follow the main county road, this time staying slightly left. Enter Fremont County; the road now is CR49. Pass under a powerline. At a third Y junction, continue south on Fremont CR49. About 9 miles from US 50, reach the Columbine trail parking area. If CR49's upper section looks too rough for your passenger car, you can park here, and take the Columbine Trail uphill for about 2.25 miles up to meet the Rainbow Trail. AWD, SUVs, and higher-clearance passenger cars can continue another 2 miles to reach the main Bear Creek trailhead. There is camping available along CR49, just past the Columbine Trail junction.

For the shorter options: From US 50/Rainbow Blvd., turn south onto Chaffee County Road 107; this intersection is one of two places along the highway with signs for "Methodist Mountain Trails." For this hike, CR107 is easier to follow than CR110 (the other route to Methodist Mountain trails). There's also a stoplight at the CR107/US 50 junction and (as of 2024) a hardware store across the highway and a burger-and-shake drive-in just east of the turn.

Drive south first on pavement, then decent dirt roads, for about 1.5 miles, staying on the main CR107 and ignoring alternatives. After 1.5 miles, CR107 magically turns into CR108. Passenger cars can drive on CR108 to an intersection with Forest Service Road 108, where they should park without blocking the road or private driveways. SUVs and better-equipped AWDs can veer left into the National Forest. AWDs may travel another 0.5 mile to a large parking/dispersed camping area on the right. AWDs should park here—yes, really. If the Forest Service gate is open, SUVs can bounce another 1 mile uphill along Loggie Gulch to intersect the Rainbow Trail as it comes in from the west (Mears Junction). For the Rainbow Trail east/Bear Creek, drive another 0.5 mile uphill, curving past buck-rail fences, to another signed trailhead.

THE HIKE: I recommend traveling west to east: you'll tackle the Poncha Mountain climb either way—but heading this direction, you should pass the hike's high point before summer afternoon thundershowers strike.

From the western trailhead, the hike climbs a moderate first mile along a seasonal creek before turning north past an aspen grove. Continue to a ridge covered in spruce-fir forest, cross the ridge, then dip under a powerline. You're now at the base of the long, steep climb around Poncha Mountain. Trudge up to the 10,250-foot-high point (about 3.6 miles from the car) and enjoy the view. Descend several miles through rolling terrain. Pass through the burned area, which opened fabulous views. Notice the great work on the rebuilt trail! At about 9 miles from your car, cross the seasonal stream in Loggie Gulch, then intersect the 4WD road.

From here, you can walk to your shuttle vehicle. If continuing, you can trek the road 0.5 mile uphill to the signed trailhead for Bear Creek.

The Columbine trail intersects the Rainbow Trail about 1.5 miles before Bear Creek.

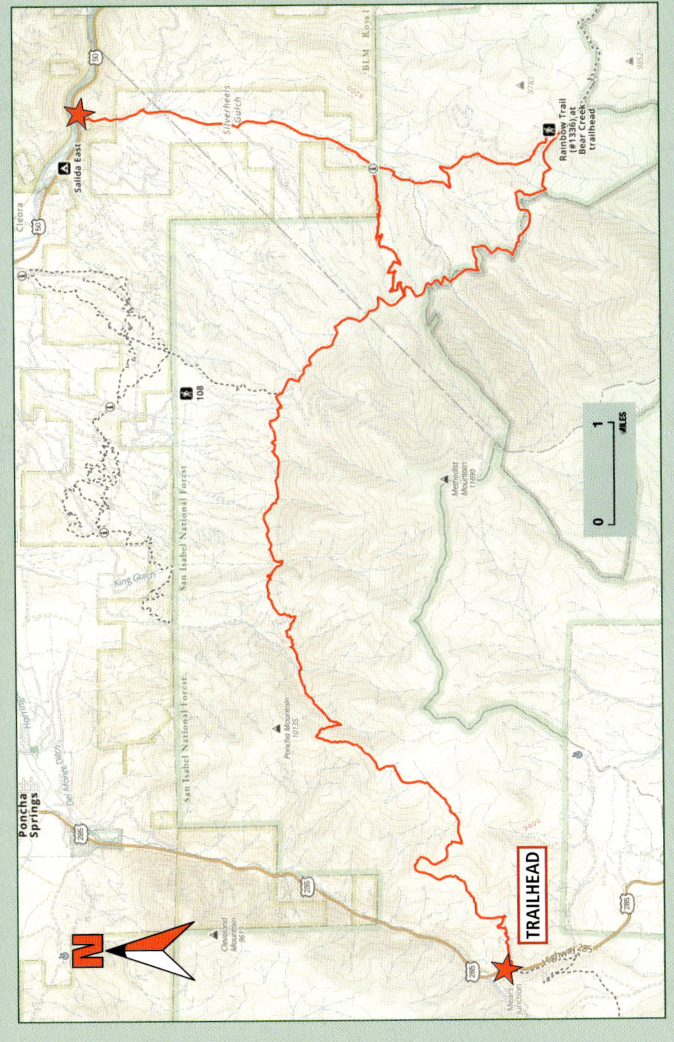
TRAILHEAD
Salida East
Poncha Springs
Silverheels Gulch
Rainbow Trail (#1336) at Bear Creek trailhead
San Isabel National Forest
Poncha Mountain 10135
Methodist Mountain 11690
Cleveland Mountain 9619
Means Junction
Highway 285
King Gulch
Cleora
108
MILES

Hikes by Difficulty

EASY

- Narrow Gauge Trail
- Interlaken
- Whipple Trail
- Harvard Lakes
- Little Rainbow Trail
- Greens Creek Trail (first mile)

MODERATE

- Waterdog Lakes
- Lake Ann
- Three Apostles Basin and View
- Browns Falls and Lake
- Wagon Loop Trail
- Greens Creek Trail (full)
- Hartenstein Lake
- Ptarmigan Lake
- Pine Creek/Bedrock Falls

DIFFICULT

- Rainbow Trail (full length)
- The Colorado Trail: Silver Creek to Avalanche Trailhead
- Continental Divide Trail/Colorado Trail Collegiate West Segment 5
- Mount Ouray
- Mount Yale
- Mount Princeton
- Mount Belford and Mount Oxford (south approach)
- Emerald and Iowa Peaks
- Mount Shavano and Tabeguache Peak
- Mount Huron

Hikes by Type

DAY HIKES

- Narrow Gauge Trail
- Interlaken
- Whipple Trail
- Harvard Lakes
- Little Rainbow Trail
- Greens Creek Trail (first mile)
- Waterdog Lakes
- Rainbow Trail (partial or in sections)
- Lake Ann (from four-wheel-drive road)
- Three Apostles Basin (from four-wheel-drive road)
- Mount Huron
- Mount Princeton
- Mount Yale
- Hartenstein Lake
- Ptarmigan Lake
- Browns Falls (to falls only)
- Wagon Loop
- Mount Shavano and Tabeguache Peak
- Little Rainbow
- Mount Ouray

BACKPACKING TRIPS

- Pine Creek/Bedrock Falls
- Emerald and Iowa Peaks
- Mount Belford and Mount Oxford (south approach)
- Greens Creek Trail (full, to the Divide)
- Browns Falls and Lake
- Continental Divide Trail/Colorado Trail Collegiate West Segment 5
- Rainbow Trail (full length)

BEST WILDFLOWER HIKES

- Pine Creek/Bedrock Falls
- Greens Creek Trail
- Waterdog Lakes
- Harvard Lakes
- Mount Yale
- Hartenstein Lake
- The Colorado Trail: Silver Creek to Avalanche Trailhead
- Boss Lake (classic approach)
- Lake Ann
- Three Apostles Basin and View
- Browns Falls and Lake
- Ptarmigan Lake

BEST BIRDING HIKES

- The entire list of wildflower hikes
- Raptors: Continental Divide Trail/Colorado Trail Collegiate West Segment 5; Rainbow Trail; Little Rainbow Trail; Lake Ann; Mount Huron
- Song birds and woodpeckers/flickers: Ptarmigan Lake; Lake Ann; Three Apostles View; Emerald and Iowa Peaks; Mount Belford and Mount Oxford; Continental Divide Trail/Colorado Trail Collegiate West Segment 5
- Ptarmigan: Ptarmigan Lake; the 13ers and 14ers above timberline; CDT/CT West Segment 5
- Pine Creek to Bedrock Falls

Reaching timberline on Mount Huron.

Acknowledgments

Several people helped me complete different parts of this book, so it's at the risk of leaving out a few folks that I extend sincere thanks to my family, for always caring about whether I return from the wilderness; Elliott Crooks, shuttle driver, camp chef, and assistant puppy wrangler; Karen Amundson, for her knowledge of the area; Brandon Hoem, for reviewing ecosystem descriptions; a longtime friend and scientist who reviewed my geologic explanations but who requested anonymity (any errors are mine alone, however); the ever-patient Jeff Golden and Sarah Gorecki, the Colorado Mountain Club's past and current publishing directors; the managers at my regular job who gave me time off so I could finish this book; and the friendly, helpful folks in Buena Vista, Salida, and surrounding communities who welcome visitors wholeheartedly.

Indian paintbrush thrives along Three Apostles Basin Trail.

About the Author

Penelope Purdy is an award-winning journalist who spent much of her career with *The Denver Post*, where she specialized in reporting about environmental issues including climate change, wildlife conservation, and national forests and parks. She continued her professional focus as a communications manager for environmental nonprofit organizations such as The Pew Charitable Trusts, a highly respected international think tank and advocacy group. Her previous guidebook, *Hiking Colorado's Roadless Trails*, also was published by Colorado Mountain Club Press.

An avid outdoorswoman, Penelope has completed the Colorado Trail and climbed all the Fourteeners in the contiguous forty-eight states including Colorado, California, and Washington state. She has climbed in the Himalayas, Andes, Canadian Rockies, and Alaska, as well as in the Rockies from Idaho to New Mexico. Penelope is a certified scuba diver, licensed private airplane pilot, certified small boat skipper, skier (downhill and cross-country), canoeist and kayaker, and a rock and ice climber. She does not like doing housework but loves endlessly cracking puns.

She earned her bachelor's degree in journalism with high honors from the University of Wyoming and her master's degree in international and intercultural communications from the University of Denver, where she also taught graduate-level classes. She now runs her own communications consulting firm for which her loveable mutt, Hitch-hiker, serves as mascot and chief morale officer.